Making Environmental Markets Work

Perhaps the most defining characteristic of the global economy today is the rise of emerging market economies (EMEs). Many of these states have experienced rapid economic growth over the past two decades that has led to an increasing share of global wealth. Such dramatic changes are highly relevant because they raise important issues about the distribution of global monetary and fiscal power. As the EMEs have gained importance in the global economy, their influence and significance have grown across a wide range of policy domains. One particularly relevant example is the increasingly critical role of EMEs in addressing climate change.

Contrary to the popular belief that the level of development determines a country's ability to produce positive environmental outcomes, this book shows that the variation in environmental outcomes among the EMEs is due, in part, to differences in the types of economic institutions prevalent in their economies. Since EMEs differ dramatically on a number of factors, examining national variations in economic institutions helps explain why international climate policy has been more successful in some countries than in others. To assess how variations in capitalism may influence important outcomes, this book explores a representative sample of thirty-one EMEs and employs a mixed-method research design that incorporates both conventional regression analysis and Qualitative Comparative Analysis (QCA) to explain these outcomes. The analysis shows that although liberal market economies were expected to perform better than other types of capitalism, their performance fell below expectations. On the contrary, economic institutions related to coordinated types of capitalism (like those found in China and Brazil) have led to greater Clean Development Mechanism (CDM) market participation.

Theoretically informed, this book employs innovative ways of understanding a broad set of increasingly important, but understudied, states in an effort to highlight the interactions found in complex socio-political and ecological systems. With the growing importance of the EMEs, a better understanding of how to design market-based policies with them in mind will be required if future efforts across a range of policy issues are to be meaningful and effective.

Tabitha M. Benney is an Assistant Professor in the Department of Political Science and affiliated faculty at the Center on Global Change and Sustainability at the University of Utah. She received her PhD in Political Science from the University of California, Santa Barbara and her MA in International Affairs from Georgetown University. Previously she worked in the Policy and Global Affairs Division of the US National Academy of Sciences (NAS) from 2002–2007. Her research interests include International Relations, International Political Economy, Environmental Politics, Global Governance and Comparative Research Methods. Professor Benney's work has been published in *Energy Policy, Wiley Interdisciplinary Reviews: Climate Change* and the *Review of International Political Economy*. She has also received numerous grants and fellowships including the Louis G. Lancaster International Relations Fellowship from 2008–2011.

Environmental Politics/Routledge Research in Environmental Politics

Edited by Steve Vanderheiden, University of Colorado at Boulder.

For a full list of titles in this series, please visit www.routledge.com

Over recent years, environmental politics has moved from a peripheral interest to a central concern within the discipline of politics. This series aims to reinforce this trend through the publication of books that investigate the nature of contemporary environmental politics and show the centrality of environmental politics to the study of politics per se. The series understands politics in a broad sense, and the books will focus on mainstream issues such as the policy process and new social movements, as well as emerging areas such as cultural politics and political economy. Books in the series will analyze contemporary political practices with regards to the environment and/or explore possible future directions for the "greening" of contemporary politics. The series will be of interest not only to academics and students working in the environmental field, but will also demand to be read within the broader discipline.

The series consists of two strands:

Environmental Politics addresses the needs of students and teachers, and the titles will be published in paperback and hardback. Titles include:

Global Warming and Global Politics
Matthew Paterson

Politics and the Environment
James Connelly & GrahamSmith

International Relations Theory and Ecological Thought
Towards Synthesis
Eric Laferrière & Peter Stoett

Planning Sustainability
Edited by Michael Kenny & James Meadowcroft

Deliberative Democracy and the Environment
Graham Smith

EU Enlargement and the Environment
Institutional change and environmental policy in Central and Eastern Europe
Edited by JoAnn Carmin and Stacy D. VanDeveer

The Crisis of Global Environmental Governance
Towards a new political economy of sustainability
Edited by Jacob Park, Ken Conca and Matthias Finger

Routledge Research in Environmental Politics presents innovative new research intended for high-level specialist readership. These titles are published in hardback only and include:

10. **The Environment and International Politics**
    International fisheries, Heidegger and social method
    Hakan Seckinelgin

11. **Postmodern Climate Change**
    Leigh Glover

12. **Contemporary Environmental Politics**
    From margins to mainstream
    Edited by Piers H.G. Stephens, with John Barry and Andrew Dobson

13. **Sustainable Consumption, Ecology and Fair Trade**
    Edited by Edwin Zaccaï

14. **Environmental Governance in China**
    Edited by Neil Carter and Arthur P. J. Mol

15. **Global Justice and Neoliberal Environmental Governance**
    Ethics, sustainable development and international cooperation
    Chukwumerije Okereke

16. **The Politics of Unsustainability**
    Eco-politics in the post-ecologist era
    Ingolfur Blühdorn and Ian Welsh

17. **International Organizations in Global Environmental Governance**
    Edited by Frank Biermann, Bernd Siebenhüner and Anna Schreyögg

18. **Regulation Theory and Sustainable Development**
    Business leaders and ecological modernisation
    Corinne Gendron

19. **International Environmental Agreements**
    An introduction
    Edited by Steinar Andresen, Elin Lerum Boasson and Geir Hønneland

20. **The Origins of Energy and Environmental Policy in Europe**
    The Beginnings of a European Environmental Conscience
    Thomas C. Hoerber

21. **Governing Social Ecological Change**
    Long-term policies
    Edited by Bernd Siebenhüner, Marlen Arnold, Klaus Eisenack, and Klaus Jacob

22. **Reforming Law and Economy for a Sustainable Earth**
    Critical Thought for Turbulent Times
    Paul Anderson

23. **Making Environmental Markets Work**
    The Varieties of Capitalism in the Emerging Economies
    Tabitha M. Benney

Making Environmental Markets Work

The Varieties of Capitalism in the Emerging Economies

Tabitha M. Benney

Routledge
Taylor & Francis Group
NEW YORK AND LONDON

First published 2015
by Routledge
711 Third Avenue, New York, NY 10017, USA

and by Routledge
2 Park Square, Milton Park, Abingdon, Oxfordshire OX14 4RN

First issued in paperback 2016

Routledge is an imprint of the Taylor & Francis Group, an informa business

Library of Congress Cataloging-in-Publication Data

Benney, Tabitha M., 1973–
Making environmental markets work : the varieties of capitalism in the emerging economies / by Tabitha M. Benney.
pages cm. — (Environmental politics/Routledge research in environmental politics ; 23)
Includes bibliographical references and index.
1. Environmental policy—Economic aspects—Developing countries. 2. Capitalism—Environmental aspects—Developing countries. 3. Developing countries—Economic policy—Environmental aspects. I. Title.
HC59.72.E5B46 2015
363.738'746091724—dc23
2014030117

Typeset in Sabon
by Apex CoVantage, LLC

ISBN 13: 978-1-138-28729-7 (pbk)
ISBN 13: 978-1-138-80698-6 (hbk)

In loving memory of Rita Benney

Contents

Figures

Tables

Acknowledgements

First and foremost I must thank Benjamin J. Cohen, Simone Pulver and Oran Young for their extended input and help with this book. All three have dedicated tremendous amounts of time and energy to helping me develop as an academic and I am eternally grateful. In addition, there have been countless people who have helped me along the way including Joe Smaldone, Tara Morton, Mary Gawronski and Jim Turner. For this book in particular, I must also give a special thanks to Patricia Bromley, Mark Button, John Foran, Nate Hultman, Garrett Glasgow, Kent Jennings, Pei-te Lien, Lorelei Moosbrugger, Neil Narang, Eric Smith, Heather Stoll and Lina Svedin for their help in getting the job done. The final and most important thank you goes to James Matthews. I literally could not have done this without him.

1 Introduction and Overview

I. INTRODUCTION AND OVERVIEW

Perhaps the most defining characteristic of the global economy today is the rise of the emerging market economies (EMEs). In fact, the aggregate output of these states has the potential to exceed that of most industrialized countries, but per capita income levels remain far lower. The rapid economic growth that results from these conditions has led to an increasing share of global wealth for many of these states. If this trend persists, we shall witness the most impressive closing of the gap between rich and poor countries in world history. Such dramatic changes are highly relevant because they raise important issues about the distribution of global monetary and fiscal power. This is especially relevant in a world where the richest states often define international policy, yet are also largely held accountable for their costs.

As the EMEs have gained importance in the global economy, their influence and significance have grown across a wide range of policy domains. One particularly relevant example is the increasingly critical role of EMEs in addressing climate change. Indeed, it is widely believed that developing countries' participation is required for a truly effective solution to global warming. This is particularly relevant now that emissions levels from the developing world are expected to outpace their post-industrial counterparts over the next three decades due to their generally stronger rate of economic growth and continued use of fossil fuels.[1] Not only are these states increasingly responsible for the ongoing problem, they also have great potential for solving it. For instance, the Organization of Economic Cooperation and Development (OECD) speculates that emissions-reducing projects in the developing world alone have the potential to contribute over 50 percent of the total emissions reductions mandated by the Kyoto Protocol (OECD 2000). Despite this great potential, most EMEs have more immediate priorities than climate change. With that in mind, a variety of international policies have been designed to directly target, incentivize and encourage the emerging economies to control their growing emissions.

One such policy was established by the United Nations Framework Convention on Climate Change (UNFCCC) under the Kyoto Protocol in 1997.

As is commonly understood, the objective of the Kyoto Protocol was to stabilize greenhouse gas (GHG) emissions at a level that would prevent dangerous anthropogenic interference with the climate system. To address its goals, the Kyoto framework required the more advanced economies (known as Annex I countries) to limit or reduce their GHG emissions. However, the industrialized world could not go it alone.

To encourage developing countries, negotiators of the Kyoto Protocol also established a global market for emissions reductions[2] through a market-based mechanism called the Clean Development Mechanism (CDM). The dual goals of the CDM are to promote sustainable development in emerging economies and to allow industrialized countries to earn emissions credits from their investments in emissions-reducing projects in developing countries. The CDM program works like a subsidy to offset the cost of pollution-reducing technologies in the developing world. By funding "green" technologies and encouraging cleaner technology updates, developing states are expected to be swayed to emit less emissions overall.

The use of markets as a means to address environmental problems is not a new idea. Economists have long encouraged the use of market-based policy instruments to address environmental problems because they are seen as a fast and efficient course of action that is capable of transcending national boundaries effectively. In reflection of this, market-based policy mechanisms like the CDM that serve to protect the environment through market principles are increasingly being advocated (Keohane and Olmstead 2007).[3]

However, little is actually understood about how such markets enable states to address environmental problems. As the CDM has run its course, responses to the policy have been extremely varied. Some countries, like China, embraced the mechanisms, whereas others, like South Africa or the United Arab Emirates (UAE), barely participated in it. With the growing importance of the EMEs, a better understanding of how to design market-based policies with them in mind will be required if future efforts across a range of issues are to be meaningful and effective. How, then, can we best account for the variations we find among the emerging economies?

This book argues that the variation in environmental outcomes among the EMEs is due to differences in the types of economic institutions prevalent in their economies. In short, it is the type of capitalism in each country that explains this outcome. This occurs because countries are comprised of varying sets of economic institutions and these institutions supply the rules of the game for how the country performs in many areas, including environmental policy. Because EMEs differ dramatically on a number of variables, national variations in economic institutions help explain why international climate policy has been more successful in some countries than in others.

A common starting point for understanding the importance of economic institutions is the work of Karl Polanyi (1944). It was Polanyi who first illustrated how the creation of capitalist institutions not only changed laws, but also molded society. He argued that with the advent of market-based institutions, human propensity to barter and trade became widespread. Since the 1940s, Polanyi's (1944) institutional approach has been borrowed, modified and elaborated on by important contemporary scholars including Andrew Shonfield (1966), Peter Katzenstein (1974, 1985), Mark Granovetter (1985) and Oliver Williamson (1985). What these scholars have helped to illustrate is that economic institutions matter because they help define the environment in which actors make decisions.

Since the 1990s, the theory of economic institutions has been extended to show that it is not one specific area of the economy that produces economic outcomes, but rather the joint effects of a series of institutions that influence the economy together (Evans 1995; Dobbin 1994; Scott 1995, 2001; Hall and Soskice 2001). These sets of institutions vary by country as a result of their unique histories and experiences. Despite the variation in their domestic institutions, states often arrive at similar outcomes in areas such as national savings rates, employment levels and even how new markets form. Understanding these sets of economic institutions can help to explain why a particular policy outcome results.

A. Goals of this Research

To better understand how sets of economic institutions influence environmental outcomes among the EMEs, this research has four main goals. The first goal is to systematically understand what the emerging economies are really like. According to the World Bank, the BRIC states (Brazil, Russia, India, China) plus South Korea and Indonesia will lead the world's economy with more than a half of all global growth by 2025 (World Bank 2011). In addition, unlike the early industrializers that took over a hundred years to mature, even the most unlikely emerging markets today have the potential to rise to the top in one to two decades. Despite this, comparative studies of market structures in EMEs are sparse, even as these states continue to play an increasing role in the world's economy. Not only are these states the future drivers of markets and policies, but their participation will be essential for solving a broad range of issues at the international level. As such, they deserve further research.

The second goal of this research is to better understand market-based policy performance. In particular, I explore what types of capitalism produced positive outcomes in the case of the CDM. To do so, I study the creation or formation of CDM markets across the EMEs beginning in 2005 when the program was implemented. This serves to inform the literature on the use of market-based policy mechanisms to resolve important global problems. By focusing attention on how best to implement such policies, this study can provide insights on the best practices for solving large-scale international problems like climate change.

The third goal of this research is to explore whether economic institutions alone determine environmental outcomes. What factors are necessary and/or sufficient for influencing EMEs in the process of market formation? Although this research assumes a rationalist approach to economic institutions, in the spirit of Karl Polanyi (1944)—it is important also to question the latent functionalism of institutionalist approaches if further inroads are to be made in the field of comparative capitalism. To address this, I explore a set of controls derived from the development literature. They include the following four variables: macroeconomic stability, infrastructure, strength of public institutions (including corruption, judicial transparency and rule of law) and the unique effects of population. Because EMEs may have different priorities from their industrialized counterparts, I aim to clarify what "other" factors matter for producing successful market-based initiatives such as the CDM. This has the potential to illustrate what motivates EMEs and how to best design market-based policies that work specifically for these states.

The final goal, which is more methodological in nature, is to demonstrate the strengths and weaknesses of mixed-method research designs for furthering our understanding of international and global politics. A particular focus of this research is to assess the effectiveness of innovative approaches, such as Qualitative Comparative Analysis (QCA)—one of the methods used in this research. QCA is an analytical technique that uses logic to derive the various pathways to a common outcome. By comparing the findings of this method with a more conventional statistical procedure, I hope to highlight important benefits of QCA that may prove fruitful for understanding how complex, socio-political and ecological systems interact.

B. Data and Methods

To achieve these goals, this book explores a representative sample of 31 EMEs to show that national variations in capitalist economies are central to explaining why CDM market formation has yielded more emissions-reducing projects in some countries than in others. The analysis for this research draws on explanatory variables from the Varieties of Capitalism (VoC) literature, which suggest that firms in capitalist economies face common problems related to labor relations, finance, inter-firm relations, education and vocational training and corporate governance (Hall and Soskice 2001). Control variables including macroeconomic stability, infrastructure, strength of public institutions and population are also considered in the analysis. These five dimensions, along with four control variables, will be operationalized to produce a series of indicators to explain the successful or unsuccessful creation of CDM markets in these states.

To analyze the data, I employ a mixed-method research design that incorporates both conventional regression analysis and QCA as complementary tools for explaining these outcomes. In doing so, I hope to illustrate the similarities and differences between these two methodological approaches. My goal is not to suggest these findings will hold across all types of research designs, but I evaluate these two methodologies across a particular type of research design—a comparative mixed-method analysis that focuses on testing asymmetric hypotheses[4] for a medium-n size sample. In such settings, QCA has important advantages when combined with conventional regression methods and together can produce more meaningful results.

C. Overview of the Book

The book is organized as follows. Chapter 2 begins with an overview of the emerging economies and the international system of classification used to label them. This chapter also explores the competing drivers of market-based environmental policies in these countries. The most common drivers or explanations for environmental outcomes focus on a country's level of development, type of political system or their national environmental values; however, these approaches may not be best suited for understanding the transboundary nature of GHG emissions in the developing world.

I begin the third chapter by introducing the comparative capitalism approach, which I argue is a more compelling explanation for the environmental outcomes found in this research. The chapter also includes a review of the VoC, which serves as the framework for this study. An overview of the relevant debates is provided, touching on issues such as the classification of capitalist types, the narrow application of the theory to industrialized states and the effect of differing types of capitalism on important outcomes such as the environment. I conclude the chapter with a brief discussion of the innovations and contributions of this research.

Chapter 4 explores how various sets of economic institutions perform in market-based policies used to incentivize new market formation. To illustrate the conceptual framework of this book the chapter begins with an overview of the CDM, the environmental policy explored in this book. Next, the definition of capitalism is conceptualized and operationalized to help establish a research protocol. The chapter concludes with a brief discussion on data sources and types.

In the second half of the book, I present my research design, analysis, findings and conclusions. Chapter 5 explores the dynamic nature of capitalism among the emerging economies. A typology is used to establish an inventory of the varieties of capitalism found among the states in my sample. I also explore which types of capitalism produce the best environmental outcomes. The chapter concludes with some thoughts on the long-running debate over the divergence or convergence of capitalist norms.

Chapter 6 provides an overview and demonstration of the QCA approach. First, a brief history of this increasingly popular method is described. The main goal of this chapter is to provide a step-by-step illustration of the QCA research process and protocol using the data for this research. Key concepts, data instruments and rules of the method are defined and illustrated.

The seventh chapter of this book explores the argument that an explanation for the success and failure of CDM market creation is likely due to the variation in capitalist institutions among the EMEs. The chapter includes an introduction of the mixed-method research design used in this research. The complementary of these two methods is also discussed. Next, I provide a comparison of the analysis produced by each method individually. I also present my final analysis of the determinates of CDM market formation.

Chapter 8 explores the findings, limitations and practical implications of this study. Contrary to the popular belief that the level of development determines a country's ability to produce positive environmental outcomes, I conclude that differences in CDM market performance (at least as it has been defined in this research) appear to be directly linked to the type of capitalism in these states. I also find that although liberal market economies were expected to perform better than other types of capitalism—because carbon markets were designed with market-based economies in mind—their performance was below expectations. Furthermore, I find that economic institutions associated with coordinated types of capitalism (like those found in China and Brazil) has led to greater CDM market participation. The underlying mechanism explaining this outcome relates to the distinct time horizon of economic decision making in the two main types of capitalism, and to how the sets of institutions within them work to facilitate the production process.

The final chapter of the book summarizes the main conclusions and provides a brief discussion on the future of this important area of research. In addition to being theoretically informed, this book presents an innovative way of understanding a broad set of increasingly important states to highlight the real interactions found within them. By mapping CDM market performance (i.e. CDM market creation) to the diversity of capitalist types, this research provides new insights into the debate over institutional influences on market behavior within emerging economies where studies remain sparse. In my research, for example, economic institutions do appear to play a central part in determining outcomes, as is predicted in the VoC theory. Nonetheless, in some cases, other factors such as high population levels and macroeconomic stability may also play a role in the success of CDM market formation. Despite this, the VoC theory remains a fruitful construct for explaining the evidence that results.

In the case of the CDM, positive performance is linked to a particular type or mode of capitalist production, which suggests that current international policy designs to address climate change may be shortsighted. If specific types of capitalism require differing forms of motivation to bring about the desired policy outcome, then current efforts to address climate change may need to adapt. Even though these findings remain preliminary, the evidence presented in this research raises important issues for further research. To address these issues, new theories, research methods, and related typologies need to be designed and tested if we are to develop a fuller understanding of how capitalism functions in various settings.

Such findings are also highly relevant for the design and implementation of other pressing policy issues, which are increasingly being addressed with the use of market mechanisms. With the growing importance of the EMEs, a better understanding of how to design market-based policies with them in mind will be required if future efforts across a range of policy issues are to be meaningful and effective. Advancing this research on market-based governance and its limitations serves to expand our long-term global governance options.

NOTES

1. According to the biennial International Energy Outlook report released by the US Energy Information Administration (EIA), "Under the policies currently in place worldwide, carbon emissions will grow 46 percent by 2040 from a 2010 baseline," which can be attributed directly to EMEs (EIA 2013).
2. Emissions markets promote the trading of GHG emissions rights. This helps to fund the reduction of GHG emissions, while also allowing actors to meet their mandated targets under the Kyoto Protocol or other cap and trade regulatory regimes.
3. Some examples including fishery permits, allocation of water rights and a range of emissions markets (Keohane and Olmstead 2007). For other examples, see Stavins (2001); Butzengeiger-Geyer et al (2011); Sovacool (2011).
4. Asymmetric hypotheses are those that study both the patterns that produce an outcome and the patterns that do not produce an outcome without the assumption that they are exact opposites. For example, in standard symmetric hypotheses, if X causes Y, then the absence of X should lead to the absence of Y. In asymmetric hypotheses, the absence of X does not necessarily suggest the absence of Y.

2 Understanding the Emerging Market Economies

Although markets have at times been the cause of environmental degradation, policy mechanisms like the emerging network of regional and international carbon markets, which serve to protect the environment through market-based principles, are gaining popularity. And due to the link between economic growth and environmental degradation, such policies are also expected to encourage growth and prosperity in the developing world while reducing impacts on the environment and human health. If applied correctly, such policies would appear to have great potential.

The reality is that little is actually understood about how such markets affect the ability of developing economies to address environmental problems. Likewise, how such policies impact human well-being and economic growth are also not well established. For example, levels of participation in emissions markets vary across emerging economies. There are several competing theories that try to explain this variation, but a lack of consensus in the literature adds to the confusion.

This chapter explores these various ideas in detail. I begin with a discussion about the Emerging Market Economies (EMEs), which is an important focus of this book. I also provide a brief introduction to the country cases used in this study. The second half of the chapter investigates three of the most common theories or drivers of environmental action—levels of development, national environmental values and types of political systems—to explain these outcomes. The aim is to provide some conclusions about their usefulness for explaining environmental outcomes in the EMEs.

In the following chapter, I will extend this discussion to introduce a fourth explanation that I see as a more promising avenue for explaining these outcomes. There, I will argue that it is the type of capitalism in each country that is central to explaining why some states have been more successful than others in addressing the very real problem of climate change.

A. THE NEW INDUSTRIALIZERS

The countries classified as "developing economies" constitute a very heterogeneous group. Within this group, there are some more advanced countries, but also a large number of poor countries. For some of these states, colonization makes up a long portion of their history, whereas others were never colonized. Understanding these differences and their underlying consequences is a central aim of this research. An important starting point for understanding the emerging economies is their unique pathway to industrialization.

The history of industrialization is best described in three main waves (Stearns 2013). The first wave, beginning in the 1770s, was led by Britain and spread to the US and a large part of Western Europe. The second wave of industrialization, which shares many similarities with the first wave, emerged around the 1880s and was centered in Russia, Japan, Southern and Eastern Europe, Canada and Australia. The third wave of industrialization first emerged in the Pacific Rim in the 1960s, and then later spread to Turkey, India, Brazil and throughout Latin America around the 1980s. The countries that have industrialized since the 1960s have done so amid a very different social, political and economic setting than the states of earlier waves. Subsequently, it seems inevitable that the industrial relations found within these states should reflect these differences.

In the first Industrial Revolution, for example, Britain began to export goods and services successfully to foreign markets, and this allowed its industries to become efficient by creating economies of scale. However, many of the recently emerging markets have followed a different path to industrialization. Instead, these states have consolidated their domestic industries prior to liberalizing their economies and this explains the rapid success of their export markets. As a consequence, emerging economies today have encouraged rapid economic growth through export-oriented industrialization. This growth-driven approach has served to insulate them from economic shocks and allowed them to dramatically reduce government deficits and debt levels over a short period of time. In addition, these countries have managed to diversify and promote innovation within their economies while simultaneously integrating into the global economy.

Because of their unique pathways to liberalization, how these economies function is not fully understood. In conjunction with this, comparative studies of market structures in the developing world are sparse. In reflection of this, my research focuses specifically on emerging states because they play an increasingly important role in the international community. By understanding the emerging economies better today, it can help guide us in understanding their evolution into the future.

Perhaps the grandest obstacle to understanding these states well is the problem of definition and classification. Although a seemingly simple problem, it is a problem that is snared by political ego and insecurity, making it at times a truly intractable problem. At the international level, the International Monetary Fund (IMF), World Bank and United Nations (UN) all have established diverse classification systems, which complicate the developing country distinction. For example, at the IMF, the country classification system divides the world into just two major groups: advanced economies and emerging and developing economies. As noted in the IMF's

World Economic Outlook Statistical Appendix, "Rather than being based on strict criteria, economic or otherwise, this classification has evolved over time with the objective of facilitating analysis by providing a reasonably meaningful organization of the data. Reclassification only happens when something marked changes or the case for change becomes overwhelming" (IMF 2012).

By contrast, the World Bank (2012) classifies countries in three ways—by region, income and by the Bank's operational lending categories (civil works preferences, International Development Association eligibility, etc.). The classification based on income is the most commonly used. It is determined by gross national income (GNI) per capita (roughly equivalent to gross national product [GNP]). Based on GNI per capita, every economy is classified as low income ($1,005 or less), middle income (subdivided into lower middle ($1,006—$3,975) and upper middle [$3,976—$12,275]), or high income ($12,276 or more). However, classification by income does not necessarily reflect development status.

The UN also classifies countries based on select economic groupings. However, according to the UN website, "There is no established convention for the designation of 'developed' and 'developing' countries or areas in the United Nations system. In common practice, Japan in Asia, Canada and the United States in northern America, Australia and New Zealand in Oceania, and Europe are considered developed regions. In international trade statistics, the Southern African Customs Union is also treated as a developed region and Israel as a developed country; countries emerging from the former Yugoslavia are treated as developing countries; and countries of eastern Europe and of the Commonwealth of Independent States in Europe are not included under either developed or developing regions" (UN 2012).

Like the main international bodies, classification also remains a problem in the private and academic sectors. In economics literature, for instance, the most common classification for economic leaders of the developing world is the term *Emerging Market Economy (EME)*. Conceptually, the EME category is a socioeconomic classification used to indicate the emerging economic status of a state. Manufacturing must account for a significant portion of the country's GDP, but otherwise, there is no formal metric used to determine if a country is an EME (Economist 2008). In general, however, these states are recently industrialized, have a strong export orientation and have high rates of growth that have allowed them to outpace other developing economies.

The EMEs as a group have received increased attention in the past two decades because of their rapidly growing share of global wealth. Such changes are highly relevant to the balance of economic power, especially in the hands of state actors who have not traditionally influenced global monetary, fiscal or other economic policies. As a simple comparison, the current size of the Brazilian economy (as measured by GDP and holding all other variables constant)[1] suggests that expansionary monetary or fiscal policy there would have a similar global impact and reach as those enacted by Spain or Canada. The impact of Indian policy would surpass that of Russia! And because the EMEs often serve as regional leaders, further understanding of how their economies work is ever more relevant in the context of the increasingly diffuse global monetary system (Cohen 2009).

However, at closer look, the term *Emerging Market Economy* is both difficult to define and outdated for operational purposes (*Economist* 2008). In fact, the varying definitions of the term produce a wide range of disparate lists. The list of EMEs prepared by Standard and Poor (2014) includes nineteen countries, whereas the Emerging Markets Index established by MasterCard includes sixty-six countries (MasterCard 2011). The problem created by this ambiguity is that some states may remain in the EME category for purely historical reasons, obscuring—for better or worse—their true status at present. In addition, many of these indices do not account for relative economic size. As a result, smaller countries with a higher productive potential are at times overlooked as an investment opportunity. This comes at a loss to investors as well as to the states it categorizes.

Consequently, the process of differentiation among emerging economies has become a highly political topic. The countries that suffer are the weaker, developing countries that are not classified as Least Developed Countries (LDCs). These countries do not benefit from any of the provisions of the LDCs, and, at the same time, they have similar commitments and obligations as the more advanced, developing countries. New, more functional differentiation among states might confer new rights for some developing states. Such rights, in the shape of special trade barriers or access to finance, could upset the balance of power in the Global South and impose distortionary impacts. However, if developing country provisions remain widespread, they also risk being counterproductive to development.

More importantly, many of the current means of classification used today are not operationally effective. For example, the commonly used classification for LDC status does not consider price or vulnerability levels within these states, making analysis of agricultural or food subsidies (a key concern in these states) impossible. The current classification systems are simply not refined enough to take true stock of a country's needs and weaknesses. Refinement is clearly required. According to a report by the Swedish Board of Agriculture, "Given that the simple systems of country classification are unable to reflect the different conditions, interests, objectives and needs of developing countries in an appropriate way, it is crucial to develop and make use of more advanced country classification systems, that are based on different relevant indicators, in order to be able to group the developing countries more appropriately with regard to the criteria we wish to analyze" (Kasteng, et al 2004, 6). Efforts to access new measures and criterion are important steps to improved operational effectiveness.

In addition to ambiguities in definition, it has become clear that the global system is no longer easily delineated along the lines of developed and developing markets anymore. Unidirectional capital flows from rich to poor countries are no longer the norm. Instead, the trend is towards countries and regions mobilizing their domestic capital resources from within their own increasingly wealthy populations. As a result, the location of capital is becoming more closely correlated with manufacturing, services and consumer locations. This is the underlying premise used to explain the success of the BRICS countries (Brazil, Russia, India, China and South Africa), for example. Considering both the literal and figurative ambiguities, it seems clear that many of the current country classification systems are outdated. Nonetheless, a new system of differentiation within the developing world is a very sensitive issue, especially for the larger and more advanced EMEs that may benefit from preserving their current status.

Case Selection

Due to the confusing and highly political nature of developing country classification, for this research I adopt the non-partisan classification system developed by the FTSE Group (2012). The FTSE Group is an independent company jointly owned by The Financial Times and the London Stock Exchange. It was established to provide objective market information and, therefore, is restricted from providing financial advice to clients. The indices established by the organization are generated by independent committees of senior fund managers, derivatives experts, actuaries and other experienced practitioners who review and approve all changes in an effort to ensure that designations are made objectively. Although the FTSE's indices are less than ten years old, they are already used extensively in a range of academic fields, including finance and management, environmental politics and gender studies.[2]

The FTSE Group has established a benchmark system to evaluate and ensure that the classification of economies in the FTSE Global Equity Index Series (GEIS) remains accurate and up to date. To do so, FTSE conducts an annual review of the market status of all countries included in this index. This process ensures that the FTSE GEIS offers the most relevant and accurate information possible about market structure, risk management and regulatory and trading practices of the economies they track.

According to the FTSE website, "The FTSE Group classifies emerging markets according to a transparent rules-based process that monitors markets status against fifteen defined Quality of Markets criteria" (FTSE 2012). The Quality of Markets criteria include six main areas of evaluation. These relate to the World Bank gross national income per capital rating, market and regulatory environment, issues surrounding custody and settlement, the business landscape, development of the derivatives market and the size of the market as determined by capitalization and market saturation. Based on these measures, each country in the FTSE GEIS index is assigned to one of three EME categories, which are distinguished as follows:

- Advanced Emerging: "Upper Middle Income GNI countries with advanced market infrastructures and High Income countries with lesser developed market infrastructures" (FTSE Group 2012).
- Secondary Emerging: "Lower Middle and Low Income countries with reasonable market infrastructures and significant size and Upper Middle Income GNI countries with lesser developed market infrastructures" (FTSE Group 2012).
- Frontier Markets: "The term frontier markets is commonly used to describe the equity markets of the smaller and less accessible, but still "investable," countries of the developing world . . . The implication of a country being labeled as frontier, or pre-emerging, is that the market is less liquid and significantly less correlated to developed and even traditional emerging markets" (FTSE Group 2012).

Because my research aims to understand markets within these three categories of countries, the specification based on market characteristics provides a practical scale by which to measure the status of these countries.

To create the sample universe for my research, I begin with all states classified by FTSE as Advanced Emerging, Secondary Emerging or Frontier Markets. By focusing on all three types of EMEs, my research avoids the important issues of comparability that inhibit some states from successful integration into global markets. As Table 2.1 illustrates, my sample universe includes ten Advanced Emerging Markets: Brazil, Czech Republic, Hungary, Malaysia, Mexico, Poland, South Africa, Taiwan, Thailand and Turkey. In addition, twelve Secondary Emerging Markets are included: Chile, China, Colombia, Egypt, India, Indonesia, Morocco, Pakistan, Peru, Philippines, Russia and the United Arab Emirates (UAE). In order to maximize variance on the dependent

Table 2.1 Sample Frame and Case Selection

Advanced EMEs		
	Brazil	
	~~Czech Republic~~	Annex I
	~~Hungary~~	Annex I
	Malaysia	
	Mexico	
	~~Poland~~	Annex I
	South Africa	
	~~Taiwan~~	Data issues
	Thailand	
	~~Turkey~~	Annex I

(*Continued*)

Table 2.1 (Continued)

Secondary EMEs		
	Chile	
	China	
	Colombia	
	Egypt	
	India	
	Indonesia	
	Morocco	
	Pakistan	
	Peru	
	Philippines	
	~~Russia~~	Annex I
	UAE	
Frontier EMEs		
	Argentina	
	Bahrain	
	Bangladesh	
	Botswana	
	~~Bulgaria~~	Annex I
	~~Croatia~~	Annex I
	Cyprus	
	~~Estonia~~	Annex I
	Jordan	
	Kenya	
	~~Lithuania~~	Annex I
	Macedonia	
	~~Malta~~	Annex I
	Mauritius	
	Nigeria	
	Qatar	
	~~Romania~~	Annex I
	Serbia	
	~~Slovakia~~	Annex I
	~~Slovenia~~	Annex I
	Sri Lanka	
	Tunisia	
	Vietnam	

variable, I also consider twenty-three Frontier Markets including: Argentina, Bahrain, Bangladesh, Botswana, Bulgaria, Croatia, Cyprus, Estonia, Jordan, Kenya, Lithuania, Macedonia, Malta, Mauritius, Nigeria, Qatar, Romania, Serbia, Slovakia, Slovenia, Sri Lanka, Tunisia and Vietnam.

The next step in the case selection process is to remove all economies that are signatories to the 1997 Kyoto Protocol as Annex I countries. Annex I countries include advanced industrialized countries and economies in transition that have ratified the Protocol and are committed to reducing their GHG emission levels. Annex I countries must be removed from my sample because they are not eligible to participate in the Clean Development Mechanism. As a result, Bulgaria, Croatia, the Czech Republic, Estonia, Hungary, Lithuania, Malta, Poland, Romania, Russia, Slovakia, Slovenia and Turkey are dropped from the sample frame. They are instead consumers of emissions credits and thus not comparable to other states in the sample. Finally, Taiwan is removed from the sample due to issues with data accessibility.

Through this case selection process, thirty-one viable cases are produced as illustrated in Figure 2.1. My final sample includes five Advanced Emerging Economies, eleven Secondary Emerging Economies and fifteen Frontier Emerging Economies.

The exclusive focus on these three types of EMEs helps to control for the level of development and is consistent with good methodological practices in both qualitative and quantitative analysis. This will help in the process of comparison between the two methodological approaches used later in this book. Despite this, some heterogeneity will inevitably result in my model due to differences that exist outside their economic standing. However, all research requires tradeoffs. For instance, if the population is limited to only Advanced EMEs, this would reduce the available degrees of freedom in statistical analysis, whereas including all developing states and trying to control for size may make identifying the causal mechanism difficult. This approach to the sample tries to balance these two demands.

B. COMPETING EXPLANATIONS FOR ENVIRONMENTAL OUTCOMES

In addition to the issue of classification, which helps to obscure a fuller understanding about what the countries in the developing world are really like, what drives environmental behavior in these states is also still largely up for debate. A big element at play here is the fact that the majority of research in this area has been focused or applied to industrialized states only. I focus on the competing explanations of environmental policies in EMEs to gain further insights into how these various drivers apply in the developing world. By improving our understanding of the unique characteristics and priorities of emerging economies, it may help us to anticipate their behavior in the future.

To understand environmental behavior in the EMEs, I start by focusing on the three main drivers of environmental outcomes found in the literature. One broadly considered driver of environmental action is the level of development—a hypothesis illustrated by the Kuznets Curve. A second approach explores the impact of national environmental values to explain these outcomes. The final approach is based on the type of political system

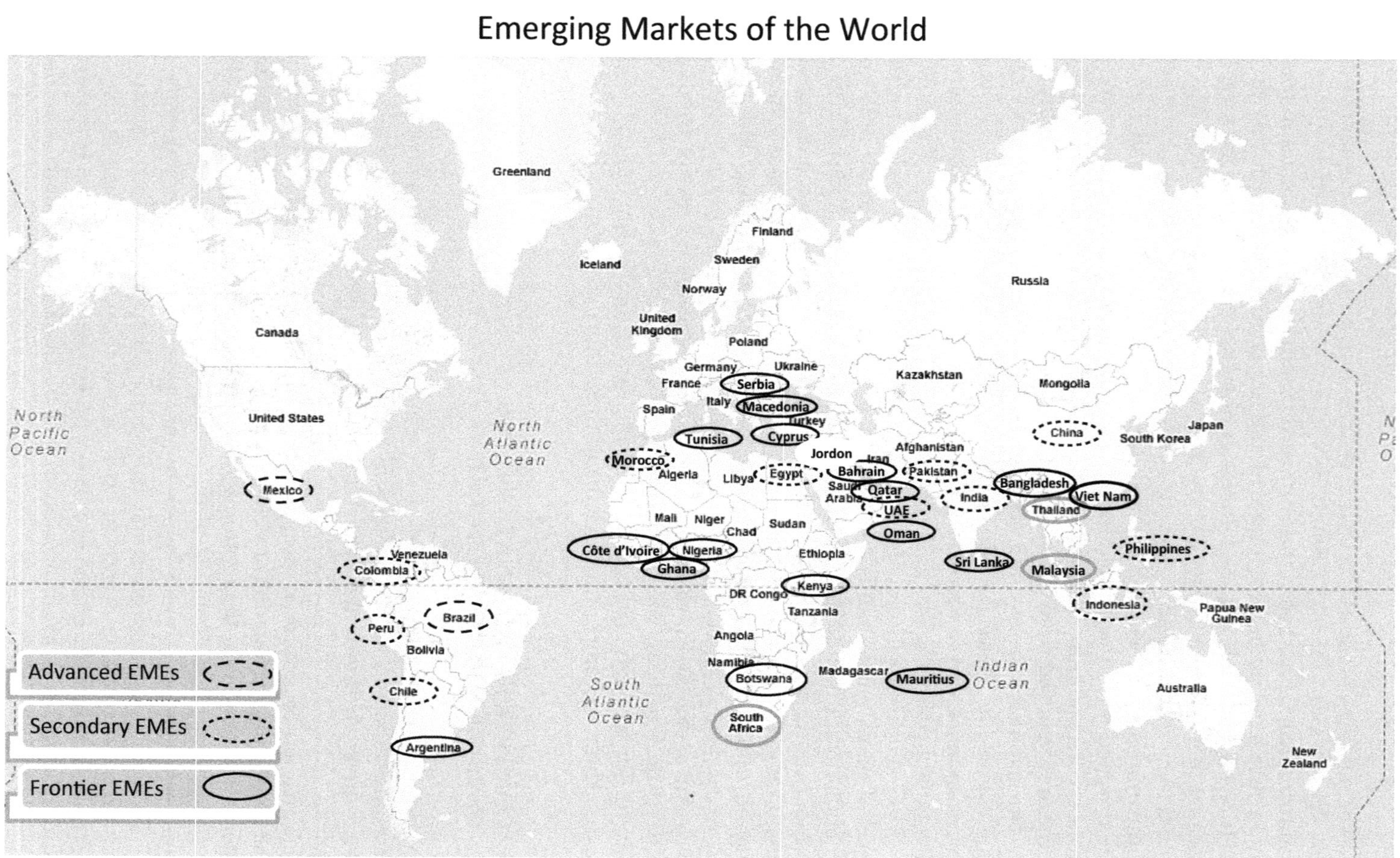

Figure 2.1 Map of the Final Case Selection

or other characteristics of the state. Although all theoretically insightful, each approach has its flaws for explaining emissions-related environmental outcomes in the EMEs. As a result, these competing explanations are less reliable for theoretically mapping policy development in this case.

Level of Development

One commonly cited driver of environmental action in the EMEs is the level of economic development. This argument was first made plain by Economist Simon Kuznets (1955) in the "Kuznets Curve." A Kuznets curve is an inverted U-shaped curve that illustrates the hypothesis that as an economy develops, a natural cycle of economic inequality occurs, driven by market forces that at first increase inequality, and then decrease it after a certain average income is attained.

Since the early 1990s, the "Environmental Kuznets Curve" (EKC) has become a standard feature in the technical literature of environmental policy (Yandle, Vijayaraghavan & Bhattarai 2000). The EKC is a hypothesized relationship between economic growth and environmental quality. The theory claims that at the beginning of industrialization, environmental damage tends to increase in response to economic growth. Once an average per capita income level is reached, environmental harms begin to decline again despite increasing growth levels (Shafik 1994).

Prior to the EKC theory, it was expected that pollution and environmental damage would grow relative to levels of economic growth. This is called the scale effect because economic development and environmental quality have traditionally been conceived as conflicting goals on opposite ends of a scale. The EKC hypothesis suggests that "at higher levels of development, structural change towards information-intensive industries and services, coupled with increased environmental awareness, enforcement of environmental regulations, better technology and higher environmental expenditures, result in leveling off and gradual decline of environmental degradation" (Panayotou 1993, 1). And whereas this sounds intuitive, it is not without problems.

Although the EKC provides a useful framework for understanding environmental quality and growth, since its early conception, it has been both theoretically and methodologically contested (Roberts and Thanos 2003). One theoretical issue of note is that the U-shaped curve is not found for all pollutants. In fact, with time, many exceptions have been noted. Some evidence supports the claim that water and airborne pollutants exhibit the inverted U-shaped curve (Yandle et al 2000). However, there is little evidence that the relationship holds for most emissions, natural resources or for biodiversity conservation (Mills and Waite 2009). For example, GHG emissions are consistently higher in industrialized countries. Those who support the theory argue that this does not weaken it, but rather shows that different environmental impacts and different regions should be expected to vary. In either event, this variability is less reliable for policy development.

A second theoretical issue up for debate is the variability of outcomes at the local versus international level. As Stern (2003) points out, many EKC studies suggest that local pollutants are more likely to display an inverted U-shape relation with income, whereas global impacts (i.e. carbon dioxide) did not. This occurs in accordance with environmental economics, which argues that "local impacts are internalized in a single economy or region and are likely to give rise to environmental policies to correct the externalities on pollutees before such policies are applied to globally externalized problems" (Stern 2003, 5). In other words, local problems are often addressed in a timely manner through policy, whereas global problems face greater collective action problems that deter quick resolution.

Yandle et al. (2000) also argue that the EKC has not been found to apply to carbon because most pollutants create localized problems like lead and sulfur, so there is a greater urgency and response to clean up such pollutants. Conversely, reducing carbon dioxide emissions does not have a dramatic impact at the local level, so the motivation to reduce them is for the sheer altruistic purpose of improving the global environment. The implication here is that the EKC theory does not provide a strong framework for understanding carbon-related emissions, especially at the international (non-local) level.

A third theoretical concern has been the lack of consensus in the field regarding the impact of trade on pollution, what is commonly known as the Pollution Haven Hypothesis. Increasing support for this concept may serve to refute the EKC theory. Suri and Chapman (1998) for example, note that industrialized states tend to export high-polluting industries to developing states that are earlier in the industrialization process. Likewise, regulation in the most developed states may also encourage the shifting of pollution production to less-regulated states (Lucas et al. 1992). In this sense, the EKC is potentially a reflection of the Pollution Haven Hypothesis.

Similarly, both Arrow et al. (1995) and Stern et al (1996) argue that the EKC is partly or largely the result of the effects of trade on the distribution of polluting industries. In particular, they cite the Hecksher-Ohlin theory that states that in a system of free and open trade, states specialize in the production of goods and services that are intensive in the relatively abundant factors of production. In the developing states, the abundant endowment would be labor and natural resources, which would encourage high intensity production activities. In the long run, impacts in the most developed states would decline, moving incrementally to the middle-income states. These interactions would exaggerate the decline in pollution intensity relative to rising income along the EKC, thus producing this effect.

In all three cases, the end result is that the total size of the negative externalities of production across time remains the same or is larger. This would explain why the more developed states follow the EKC and why developing states do not. If there is enough variability between states, allowing the former developing state to pass along the polluting industry to the next generation of developing states, this might also help to explain why EKCs are only applicable to certain types of pollutants (Yandle et al. 2000).

Methodological, there are also some weaknesses to this approach. For example, David Stern (2003) presents a variety of evidence that shows that the statistical analysis on which the EKC is based is not robust. He finds that when appropriate statistical tests and techniques are used, the EKC does not exist (Perman and Stern 2003). Instead, Stern attributes this to time-related effects that reduce environmental impacts in countries at all levels of income. However, "in rapidly growing middle income countries, the scale effect, which increases pollution and other degradation, overwhelms the time effect. In wealthy countries, growth is slower, and pollution reduction efforts can overcome the scale effect. This is the origin of the apparent EKC effect" (Stern 2003, 1).

A second methodological weakness is that the EKC model assumes linearity. For example, Arrow et al. (1995) show that the EKC model assumes that there is no feedback from environmental damage to economic production as income is assumed to be an exogenous variable. The assumption is that environmental damage does not detract from future economic productivity. In reality, we know that just the opposite is occurring. Today in China, for example, it is estimated that the cost of air pollution alone consumes one to four percent of GDP annually (Gallagher & Lewis 2012).

As Oran Young (2013) and others have recently reminded us, modeling biophysical systems or socioeconomic systems alone is challenging enough. But socio-ecological systems are far more complex and dynamic than anything we have encountered previously. In addition to being complex, the systems we use to manage human-environment interactions are highly dynamic. They change continually, and we cannot expect homeostatic processes to preserve them. Such systems are also considered nonlinear—meaning that they are constantly changing and sometimes these changes seem sudden or abrupt in character. But it is the shifting rate of change, rather than the speed of change, that is important with regard to (non)linearity. If we use simple assumptions that do not reflect the realities of the system, we will never move on from the belief that environmental degradation will not impact economic growth or human well-being.

A final methodological debate questions the validity of this theoretical framework over time. The EKC approach poses the concerning question of whether pollution actually begins to decline for good when an economic threshold is reached, or whether the decrease is only in local pollutants and pollution is simply exported to poorer developing countries. In both scenarios, the EKC may not be detectable for the states in my sample because the patterns of pollution may not be passed on from many of these states. In that case, the EMEs may not be well supported by this approach.

As a quick review of the literature, this classic approach has some particular weaknesses that do not support the study of emissions policies at the international level. One difficulty with this model is that it lacks predictive power because it is highly uncertain how the next phase of economic development will be characterized. My research, as I will demonstrate in the next chapter, also suggests that all three levels of EMEs are capable of producing successful environmental outcomes. This implies that success or failure does not appear to be a function of the level of development. Therefore, it makes sense to argue that environmental outcomes cannot simply be explained away by a country's level of development.

National Environmental Values

More recent work in political science, sociology and environmental politics has also taken the time to explore the impact of national environmental values on environmental outcomes. According to Thomas Dietz, Amy Fitzgerald, and Rachael Shwom (2005), "in the behavioral sciences, two major lines of research have addressed environmental values. One has focused on four value clusters: self-interest, altruism, traditionalism, and openness to change and found relatively consistent theoretical and empirical support for the relationship of values to environmentalism. The other line of research suggests that environmentalism emerges when basic material needs are met and those individuals and societies that are post materialist in their values are more likely to exhibit pro-environmental behaviors" (335). The first of the two approaches, although useful theoretically, is difficult to measure objectively. The overall evidence in the second approach, however, is even less compelling. There are clear connections to environmental concerns, but little is understood about the causes of value change and the overall effects of value change on behavioral change.

In environmental sociology, for instance, there is a debate about the extent to which concern about environmental problems is a result of the objective deterioration of environmental conditions or subjective values among environmentally oriented individuals—also known as the post-materialist values explanation (Running 2012). In Katrina Running's study (2012), she tests forty-four countries across various levels of development using data from the 2005–2008 World Values Survey and the Climate Risk Index to evaluate "concern for global warming" and "prioritization of environmental protection" (2012, 6). The goal is to understand whether a country's level of economic development affects these outcomes. Her findings suggest that the objective explanation of environmental concern does not apply well in any country category, but that post-materialist values do increase the odds that individuals consider global warming to be a very serious problem. However, this is clearly not a characteristic of EMEs, but rather a factor found in countries at the most advanced stage of economic development. For the EMEs, this effect is not all that useful from an analysis perspective.

The real strength of the national values approach is that as environmental issues become increasingly salient, understanding how economic development status conditions environmental concern could improve international efforts to address climate change and other global environmental problems. Nevertheless, this approach has some general issues that make it somewhat less useful for understanding environmental outcomes in EMEs specifically.

First, it is difficult to map causal relationships in value-based interactions. Many environmentally consequential behaviors are strongly influenced by factors outside an individual's control. Besides structural determinants of environmental decisions, interactions with others and the social context within which we are embedded also matters. Gregory Guagnano, Paul Stern and Thomas Dietz (1995) offer an "Attitudes-Behaviors-Constraints" theory of pro-environmental behavior that emphasizes the interaction between attitudes and constraints in shaping behavior. The key insight from their work is that research findings in this area may be inconsistent because researchers do not take adequate account of both attitudes and constraints as influences on behavior.

Another common critique is that values-based relationships are not valid or reliable measures of consumer or political action (Vig and Kraft 2013; Chasek et al. 2014). If we use the selected sample of EMEs in this book, they provide a useful example for illustration. According to the World Values Survey (2013) for the years 2005–2008, in the question about the "seriousness of climate change" only twenty-nine percent of the cases from this sample had policies that reflected the environmental value espoused in the survey question. In this case, only three successful cases, (Argentina, Brazil and India) and two failed cases (Malaysia and Thailand) are correctly correlated. The remaining states available for the specified time frame are labeled incorrectly—meaning the strength and value of their support for climate action is not reflected in either their political action or their physical reduction of emissions. Although this is just one example, it fits with a greater pattern that is well documented in the literature.

This leads to a final, but important, aspect about this literature in general. National Values Surveys relating to environmental issues tend to use abstract concepts, which are generally accepted as approximations. Some very detailed methodologies have been developed over time, particularly relating to the CDM, but in general, the validity of these measures can be weak and lack generalizability. This is not to suggest that surveys are not extremely useful, but rather that they are most useful for understanding perceptions about relevant scenarios. Often, this is done using revealed preference models that estimate how people value a particular aspect of an environmental amenity from their actual behavior, as revealed in markets. To assess this, studies are designed to determine a society's willingness to pay for improvements in environmental quality or natural resource amenities. Thus an important limitation of the values-based literature is that very few studies examine actual behavior, and the link between self-reported behavior and actual behavior is far from perfect (Dietz et al 2005, 338).

Types of Political Systems

A third well-understood driver of environmental action in EMEs is based on the type of political system or other characteristics of the state. In many cases, efforts have been made to tie various regime types to environmental outcomes. However, the empirical evidence on national environmental performance (Neumayer 2002; Esty and Porter 2005 and Li and Reuveny 2006), and national climate performance among democratic and nondemocratic states is ambiguous (Congleton 1992; Midlarsky 1998; Roberts et al. 2004; Gleditsch and Sverdrup 2003, and Battig and Bernauer 2009). In an earlier work by Robyn Eckersley (2004), she concluded that there is no evidence in the literature to support the proposition that nondemocratic regimes are better equipped than democratic ones to enact and implement robust climate policies.

Beyond regime type, other characteristics of the state have also been considered. The various indicators used to measure state performance are quite varied and complex. Primary measures often include regime type, domestic political institutions, national interests, national discourses, economic systems and domestic actors (especially those with some form of special influence or veto ability).

An essential review of this literature by Peter Christoff and Robyn Eckersley (2011), entitled "Comparing State Responses," provides a critical overview of research on comparative state responses to the challenge of climate change. The authors argue that whereas there does appear to be some clear characteristics of states (e.g. strong leadership of the political executive, advanced economy, strong civil society, a strong and respected tradition of R&D and diverse media) that can improve performance of environmental outcomes, just the opposite characteristics may also be successful (i.e. China). Perhaps their most significant finding is that "inevitably these rankings are determined by what is measured" (Christoff and Eckersley 2011, 432). In other words, despite significant institutional differences, the various typologies across fields do not produce a reliable set of determinates for identifying leaders in environmental performance.

In addition to a general lack of theoretical consensus in this approach, methodologically, it is also hard to specify in a meaningful way. This explains why it is often more difficult to evaluate as a policy. For example, reducing emissions can be caused by well-devised policies or an accidental recession, depression or a national tragedy, as illustrated by the global economic downturn in 2008. Furthermore, a lack of standards for measuring and comparing such regulation across countries illustrates the lack of consensus about the "meaning of equity, differentiated responsibilities, [and] capability under Articles 3(1) [of Kyoto Protocol]. This has prevented the determination of a single, principled approach to the allocation of mitigation obligations to individual states and left it instead to individual countries to determine their own 'equitable share' of global effort" (Christoff and Eckersley 2011, 432). Thus, this approach ignores a variety of other factors that might be at play.

Throughout the world, environmental degradation is a growing concern. To address these problems, an increasingly common solution is the use of market-based policies. Building a better understanding of how to support such markets will be required as their use gains popularity. The challenge to policy makers, then, is to improve their design and implementation or determine once and for all that such efforts are not useful at the international level.

Through a comparison of three commonly used drivers of environmental outcomes, my research suggests that success and failure of CDM uptake in EMEs is not well explained by a country's level of development, environmental values or political type. Although each is theoretically insightful, these approaches each have flaws that dampen their ability to explain emissions related environmental outcomes in the EMEs at the international level. Furthermore, I find that countries from all three levels of emerging economies, regime type and values levels are capable of producing successful CDM markets. To address this, new theories, research methods and related typologies need to be designed and tested if we are to get a fuller understanding of how environmental markets function.

NOTES

1. Other critical variables such as the degree of openness and the composition and direction of trade relations are also relevant in determining the economic capabilities of an economy. This example is merely a means to recognize the growing influence and potential of these states.
2. For examples, see the following: Singh and Vinnecombe (2005); Mase (2007) and Currana and Moranb (2006).

3 Theories of Comparative Capitalism

As Garrett Hardin (1968) established in the "Tragedy of the Commons," the environment is a common good. It is shared by all and owned by none. In the past, most environmental goods were considered inexhaustible, but today we understand that natural resources are susceptible to overuse because property rights and political freedoms rationally drive individuals to consume as much as they can, and pay as little as possible for it. This excessive overuse by rational market actors is considered a market failure. In this case, uncoordinated or underregulated markets driven by agents working in their own self-interest fails to manage these goods in optimal quantities. Despite this, economists have urged the use of market-based policies, such as emissions trading, to address environmental problems for some time. Because markets are notorious for overusing common goods, should they be applied to all areas of public policy?

As the previous chapter concluded, environmental drivers such as the level of development, national values and types of political systems, although useful in some areas, have not been strongly linked to transboundary environmental problems, especially in the developing world. To address this, I argue that a comparative-capitalism approach is more useful for understanding why some countries embrace market-based environmental policies, whereas others barely participated in them. This approach holds more merit theoretically because economic activity and production processes have been strongly linked to emissions-related environmental outcomes at the international level.

To introduce this approach, the chapter begins with a brief discussion on comparative capitalism. Next, I describe the Varieties of Capitalism (VoC) approach, which serves as the framework of this study. I also explore the related critiques and debates in the literature, which includes the classification of capitalist types, its focus on industrialized states and the effect of differing types of capitalism on important outcomes such as growth, innovation or the provision of common goods. In particular, I focus on the recent application of this body of literature as a possible driver of environmental outcomes, especially those that apply to international emissions markets and emerging economies. I conclude the chapter with a brief discussion on the contributions of this research.

A. COMPARATIVE CAPITALISM

In recognition of the link between production processes and environmental harms, it makes sense to consider how environmental outcomes may be attributed to the system of accumulation found within a state. This is reflected well within the literature on comparative capitalism where there is a broad debate about the effects of institutional variations in contemporary capitalist economies. Such variations occur because numerous social, economic and political factors constitute a state's institutional structure. Each unique institutional structure provides firms with advantages or disadvantages for engaging in specific types of activities (Scott 1995). For example, multinational corporations (MNCs) operating in different countries with varying institutional environments face diverse pressures that produce differing performance outcomes. From this it can be inferred that firms in different types of economies react differently to similar challenges.

Whereas the literature suggests that different institutional arrangements produce distinct strengths and weaknesses in the types of economies they produce, research on how this applies to environmental goods has only recently gained traction with the increasing concern over climate change. Subsequently, international economic and environmental institutions have often been analyzed in isolation, but emerging research on institutional linkages illustrates the multitude of complex relationships between them. Consequently, environmental outcomes within national economic systems are increasingly seen as being shaped by distinct institutional configurations that cause a particular logic of economic action. It is from this perspective that this chapter proceeds.

Although institutional theory (Hall and Taylor 1996; Scott 2001) is foundational to the growing field of comparative capitalism, research in this area is also drawn from institutional economics (Polanyi 1944; Williamson 1981; 1985; North 1990; Ostrom 2007), political science (Katzenstein 1974; Young 1989, 2008; Hoffman 2003; Mitchell 2009) and economic sociology (DiMaggio and Powell 1983; Granovetter 1985; Evans 1995). Although the subject is interdisciplinary with a wide range of analytical and theoretical influences, there are some common assumptions. The main idea is that the institutions of capitalism differ across countries and that these differences are not coincidental, but rather are consequential.

The comparative capitalism approach is explicitly concerned with issues of competitiveness at firm, sector and national levels and has been praised for its ability to avoid single definitions of competitiveness. According to Green, et al (2010, 19), "One of the strengths of the literature is its commitment to analyzing competitiveness at different levels, and, more importantly, to revealing the articulation between firm-level and state strategies on which competitiveness partly depends." In fact, the explicit aim to compare and contrast the different national systems of competitiveness helps to avoid the narrowness of a single definition. By incorporating a broad range of measures for national economic performance, a more comprehensive approach to measuring capitalism is produced.

Early conceptions of comparative capitalism focused on mapping the diversity of national approaches to governing economic activity. The first application of this approach was used to distinguish between two different versions of modern capitalism. The first was described as the flexible and individualistic Anglo-Saxon model, which aimed to maximize profits in the short-term. The second type identified was the "Rhenish" model of capitalism. This type was characterized by long-term commitments and the highest possible consensus among actors within the economic system (Albert 1991).

These nascent efforts later evolved to produce what Richard Whitley (1992) called a fivefold classification of "business systems," which was based on how economic activity is governed. A business system, as Whitley defined it, was considered a pattern of economic organization that varied in degree and mode of authoritative coordination. Such patterns included governance by markets, hierarchies, the state, networks or business associations. "These are, with examples, centrifugal (Chinese family business), partitioned (Anglo-Saxon), collaborative (Germany), coordinated (Japan) and state-dependent (South Korea)" (Radice 2000, 726).The expanded system of classification began a debate as to what accounts for the remaining variance in capitalist societies outside these general distinctions.

By the early 1990s, a fresh wave of interest in the comparative capitalism approach emerged. This revival has largely been attributed in the differences in the performances of Germany and Japan (seen as one type) and the US and the United Kingdom (seen as a second type) following the economic downturn starting in the 1970s and the apparent reversal of these outcomes in the early 1990s. Here, the comparative capitalism approach provided a compelling argument by illustrating how enduring institutional differences gave rise to different logics of action within distinct national institutional contexts (Jackson and Deeg 2006).

The question about the functional differences involved in distinguishing types of capitalism produced two main streams of analysis (Hollingsworth and Boyer 1997). The first explored the degree to which power is distributed horizontally or vertically within the system. For example, Hart (1992) argues that differences in national performance are largely shaped by the contrasts in the distribution of power among governments, business and labor. The second stream began to explore the agency or the degree of self-interest of firms within an economic system and voiced concerns about how they might behave in an increasingly globalized system (Berger and Dore 1996; Crouch and Streeck 1997). In the edited volume by J. Rogers Hollingsworth, Philippe C. Schmitter, and Wolfgang Streeck (1994), for example, the authors demonstrate how variation in state policies influence the performance of industrial sectors and conclude that tightly controlled sectors outperform their less-regulated counterparts in the world economy. Together, these two streams of analysis helped to produce a well-articulated body of research.

B. THE VARIETIES OF CAPITALISM (VoC) APPROACH

By the late 1990s, a consensus began to form within the comparative capitalism literature that led to what is often referred to as the VoC approach. Central to this body of scholarship is the foundational work by Peter Hall and David Soskice (2001). The VoC approach uses firm-level analysis to explain state outcomes because firms are seen as the main actors in ordering a capitalist economy and are often aggregated to indicate the overall economic performance of the state. This is similar to the idea of a trade balance. Although we might say that the US has a trade deficit, it is not necessarily the state itself that has caused that imbalance. In reality, the imbalance can be attributed to the buying and selling of goods and services by consumers and firms within the economy, which produces this deficit in the short-term.

Hall and Soskice's (2001) firm-centered political economy is based on a relational view, "one in which the firms develop their core competencies and dynamic capabilities by coordinating effectively in five spheres" (Coates 2002, 467). These five spheres include labor relations, finance, inter-firm relationships, education and vocational training as well as corporate governance (Hall and Soskice 2001). It is the relationship between and among these spheres and the firm that is argued to characterize the outcomes found within a state. Coordination in these spheres occurs uniquely in each type of capitalism by giving firms a comparative institutional advantage if they exploit the unique strengths of the national system in which they find themselves embedded.

In contrast to previous approaches, the work by Hall and Soskice (2001) provides an explanation for cross-national differences in firm behavior that is based on institutional complementarity. They argue that understanding the diversity of institutional structures, and hence the diversity of capitalist societies, requires the study of how different institutions are complementary to each other. Two institutions can be defined as complementary if the presence of one increases the efficiency or returns from the other (Hall and Soskice 2001, 17). Complementary institutions make one another more or less efficient according to their respective characteristics, but functional sets of institutions tend to be enduring and outlive dysfunctional ones.

When sets of stable institutions combine, they develop into a coherent pattern. For example, short-term finance requires fast entry and exit from markets and industrial relations are most effective when quick and cheap hiring and firing of employees is possible. In such cases, it is expected that one institution functions all the better because some other institutions or forms of organization are present. Several sets of institutions taken together reinforce each other so that they form a coherent and stable, but not unchanging, structure. Once firms become embedded in the institutional subsystems that shape their particular capitalist model, they mutually reinforce one another. This structure, which varies by country, shapes the general features of the economy. With time, these social forms are secured and maintained by institutionalized value systems and intersubjective understanding rather than by power-based rules and material capabilities alone (McKenzie 2008).

Because different sets of institutions and therefore institutional complementarities are possible, this means that multiple pathways to a common outcome are possible. In short, different sets or structures of institutions may perform equally well in spite of being comprised of very different institutions and how they operate together. The final result is that firms in diverse economies react differently to similar challenges. Proceeding from this starting point, Hall and Soskice (2001) established their theory of comparative institutional advantage and institutional path dependence.

The basis for the logic of institutional behavior is fairly well understood. At the national level, economic institutions matter because they partly and imperfectly solve problems of economic coordination among agents that in turn determine outcomes like savings rates, how capital accumulates, etc., all of which govern a country's economic growth and prosperity. The sets of economic institutions that make up the state influence firm behavior by defining the incentive framework in which agents make decisions. It is therefore logical to take into account the structure formed by these institutional arrangements and argue that this institutional structure defines the behavior of each type of capitalism it produces. This also helps to explain the existence of varying institutional types for modern capitalism.

Based on this logic, Hall and Soskice (2001) specified two ideal types of capitalism that were distinguished by the degree of coordination that exists within an economy. They identify the liberal market economy (LME) and the coordinated market economy (CME), which are diametrically opposed along all institutional subsystems.

The LME ideal type is defined by "conflict susceptible management-labor relations, short-term employment, the predominance of financial markets for corporate financing, an active market for corporate control, and a strong emphasis on short-term price movements in the stock market" (Hall and Soskice 2001, 21–27). Comparative advantages for the LME model are in sectors with radical and capital-intensive innovation like biotechnology or high-end services.

In contrast, the characteristics of the CME model are a consensual relationship between capital, organized labor associations and the provision of long-term capital by major banks. "Stable ownership grants firms considerable protection against hostile takeovers. All of these factors support long-term investment in human resource development, which is crucial for the CME specialization in highly skilled and quality products based on incremental innovation" (Hall and Soskice 2001, 27–33). Together, these ideal types defined the degree of coordination that exists within capitalist economies under the original VoC approach.

C. CRITIQUES AND DEBATES IN THE LITERATURE

Currently, the VoC approach has evolved into a mature and well-articulated research framework. Numerous studies exist that employ this approach and others analyze the various institutional subsystems that compose it.[1] Nonetheless, as with all social, scientific pursuits, several debates have emerged. In particular, there are three especially intractable debates that animate the field. First is the issue of how to classify economies and the number of different varieties of capitalism that result from the various classifications. Another important criticism of the VoC approach is that it has been limited to the analysis of countries that are members of the Organization for Economic Cooperation and Development (OECD). Finally, there remains some debate about the effects that the various forms of capitalism might have on key outcomes such as growth, competitiveness, innovation and the provision of public and common goods.

The Classification of Capitalism

Inevitably, a major point of contention in this literature relates to the logic behind the classification of economies and over the number of different capitalist types. For instance, Hall and Soskice (2001) adopted a binary approach contrasting LMEs and CMEs. Many other writers in the field have used similar binary models. Dore (2002) contrasts the "relational capitalism" associated with Germany and East Asian states, with the "stockholder capitalism" of the UK and the US. Hutton (1995, 1999, 2002) contrasts the "shareholder capitalism" of the liberal market economies with the "stakeholder capitalism" of the social market economies in northern continental Europe, including Scandinavia. The economies of southern Europe are seen as permutations of the social market or stakeholder model (Amable 2003).

Some approaches find at least three dominant models in the West (Green, Preston and Janmaat 2006; Schmidt 2002; Pontusson 2005). Pontusson (2005), for instance, argues that the Nordics cannot and should not be considered as coordinated economies because of a number of unique characteristics they retain. Other scholars exploring regulation theory have made classifications with up to six models of capitalism (Hollingsworth and Boyer 1997; Amable 2003). Finally, Casey (2007) depicts some variations within the LME model that differentiate the UK from other liberal economies such as the US.

Likewise, the reliance on two ideal types of capitalism becomes problematic when analyzing countries where the state plays a central role in shaping the economy. An early example of this concept was well articulated in the contemporary writings of Frank Dobbin (1994), who explored early railroad policies in the US, UK and France. In his work, Dobbin (1994) argued that the industrial policies of various countries differ from each other, but this variation was a reflection of how political power is organized there.

In this same vein, Vivien Schmidt (2002) has identified a so called *state-enhanced market economy*, drawing on empirical evidence from France and Italy. In these countries, the business relationship tends to be state-organized, and industry is more dependent on the state than on banks or bond markets for financing. Furthermore, the state may also influence business development and wage bargaining (Schmidt 2002). As a consequence,

Schmidt proposes a distinction among three models of capitalism: market, managed and state capitalism (Schmidt 2001, 2003). Such distinctions are ever more relevant due to the important role that government has played in the export-driven industrializers that are emerging today.

Focus on Industrialized States

One of the most important points of criticism of the VoC approach is that it has been limited to the analysis of countries that are members of the OECD. Initially, the VoC literature focused on comparisons between Anglo-Saxon and continental European capitalism (Lazonick 1992; Whitley 1992; Stallings and Streeck 1995; Hollingsworth and Boyer 1997; Lazonick and O'Sullivan 2002). With only a few exceptions, countries in Africa, Latin America and other non-OECD countries have received little attention, until very recently (Phillips 2004, Feldmann 2006). In Eastern Europe, for example, few studies exist that try to identify a specific institutional configuration of capitalism there. Research in this area is limited to theoretical work (Lane and Myant 2007), single-case studies (Buchen 2004; Mykhnenko 2007) or single institutional subsystems, such as industrial relations in East Germany (Piore and Sabel 1984) or among former Soviet states (Feldman 2006). More recent scholarship focuses on Southern European capitalism (Rangone and Solari 2009), but has otherwise been limited.

With the very recent rise of China, the story in Asia has only recently started to be analyzed. Prior to 2009, and with the exception of the work by Peter Evans (1995), the few studies that dealt with economic institutions in Asian countries were almost solely focused on Japan, which serves as an ideal type for CMEs (Yamamura and Streeck 2001; Dore 1996; Vogel 2006). The VoC approach was later applied to examining the divergent trajectories of the East Asian tigers (Haggard 1990; Evans 1995; Weiss 1998; Yeung 2000), but otherwise, few advances occurred for some time. Some single-case studies were done on China (Ahrens and Jünemann 2007), South Korea (Chang 2003) and Vietnam (Chand, Duncan & Quang 2001), but they were rare.

After the global economic downturn in 2008, however, a resurgence of work on the varieties of capitalism in Asia emerged. This began with a special edition of the *Asia Pacific Journal of Management* in 2009. Michael Carney, Eric Gedajlovic and Xiaohua Yang (2009) introduce the special edition and examine the extent to which the VoC model can be fruitfully applied in the Asian context. The application of cases within this special edition alone diverges dramatically from past work in this area. Articles in this edition include single-case studies on China (Redding and Witt 2009; Tan and Zeng 2009), pair-comparisons in Taiwan and Korea (Dodgson 2009) and Thailand and Malaysia (Andriesse and van Westen 2009) as well as regional studies (Tipton 2009; Ritchie 2009; Heugens, van Essen and van Oosterhout 2009; Siri Terjesen and Jolanda Hessels 2009)—that focus on aspects of the VoC approach in Asia.

Since this time, several well-established authors from the field have also taken on this theme. For example, Neil Fligstein and Jianjun Zhang (2011) published a highly cited piece on Chinese capitalism that uses the comparative capitalism approach. Then in 2012, Andrew Walter and Xiaoke Zhang (2012) edited a book called *East Asian Capitalism: Diversity, Continuity and Change*, which focuses on capitalist systems in China, Japan, South Korea, Indonesia, the Philippines, Malaysia, Taiwan and Thailand. Most recently, *Socioeconomic Review* also produced a special journal edition entitled, "Bringing Asia into the Comparative Capitalism Perspective" (Storz, Amable, Casper, and Lechevalier 2013). The overarching theme of this volume is to consolidate and extend our understanding of both the institutional variety within and common patterns of economic coordination across Asia.

A common finding in many of these works is that these late industrializers are unique from past ideal types. Dr. Myung-koo Kang of Stanford University (2008) supports this, arguing that comparative analysis in Asia is less effective as an approach there because each country developed substantially different models of economic development and reforms due to their unique institutional settings and sociopolitical contexts. Ritchie (2009) also argues that due to their later industrialization, the traditional VoC ideal types do not hold in Southeast Asian states. He argues that a "State Coordinated, Liberal Market Economy" type has emerged, which combines aspects of the LME, CME and development state model. Peck and Zhang (2013) even question the extent to which the Chinese economy can be meaningfully characterized as capitalist due to the character of its state form, its recent development path and its position within—or beyond—conventional understandings of capitalist variety.

Moreover, in the most recent attempts to apply the VoC approach in Latin America (Schneider 2009; Schrank 2009), some authors agree that the standard ideal types do not hold up. In the work by Ben Ross Schneider (2009), for example, additional "spheres" are considered and a new ideal type called the "Hierarchical Market Economy" is proposed. Schneider contends that this new ideal type is required to take into account the distinguishing features of Latin American business groups and the large influence of foreign MNCs there.

Peck and Zhang (2013) are not alone is suggesting that the VoC theory is not suitable for understanding the emerging and developing economies. The introduction of ad hoc ideal types and the lack of consensus on the model outside the OECD states suggest that the VoC model is not viable, or at best, lacks generalizability to all capitalist states. For instance, Matthias Ebenau (2012) recently critiqued the application of the VoC model in Latin America and argues that the approach is lacking for analysis in the developing world because it cannot fully account for all inputs there. Patterns do not match up and worse, do not help to inform or overcome the weaknesses exposed there. He concludes that such scholarship is merely a form of "methodological nationalism."

OUTCOMES OF CAPITALISM

Finally, there remains some debate about the effects that the various forms of capitalism might have on key outcomes such as growth, competitiveness, innovation and the provision of public and common goods. A particularly relevant subset of this debate focuses on the nexus between the comparative analysis of capitalism and the emergence of environmental markets. This includes research on the Sociology of Markets, Varieties of Carbon Governance—a global governance theme—and the most recent work on how the variety of capitalism influences the manner in which states address climate change.

The Sociology of Markets, for example, is a well-defined research program that uses a complex, multidisciplinary framework to understand the genesis and maintenance of markets, especially those related to the growing problem of climate change. A common theme of this work is the embedded nature of market formation (Granovetter 1985). The sociological framework used in this work helps to explain the social processes inherent in this topic. For example, market formation is considered a social process that is first defined by regulation and then intersubjectively established and institutionalized.

The related works from the Sociology of Markets literature focus on two important aspects of market formation. The first aspect is the organizational basis of market formation. Here, markets are studied as social institutions that are designed for a specific task—in this case, to help reduce or at least regulate emissions. For example, in the article "The Contours of Cap and Trade" by Michele Betsill and Matthew Hoffmann (2011), the authors document the evolution of "cap and trade" along spatial, temporal, and institutional dimensions as a policy response to global climate change. The result of this process is a complex network of governance that has remained contested and unresolved on many levels. Betsill and Hoffmann (2011) argue that such contestation demonstrates the need for greater incorporation or attention to the socio-political nature of cap and trade markets and the policies they involve.

Perhaps the most articulate author in this area is Janelle Knox-Hayes (2009, 2010). In her article entitled, "Creating the Carbon Market Institution: Analysis of the Organizations and Relationships that Build the Market," she explores the development of emission markets from an institutional perspective to understand how market networks and related institutions are constructed. To do so, she shows how various public and private organizations, rather than regulatory bodies, build the institutions of the carbon market. Together, these actors develop the regulative, normative and cultural "pillars" necessary for carbon market formation. She contends that "[s]ince organizations build the institutional pillars of the carbon market network, the strength of the institution cannot be determined by regulation alone. Certainly regulation gives the carbon markets credibility, but their ability to become an institution of common practice relies on the strength and embeddedness of the organizations that build them" (Knox-Hayes 2010, 176).

The second related aspect drawn from the Sociology of Markets literature focuses on the social process of commoditization. Here, efforts have been made to illustrate how an intangible good is commoditized and rationalized in an effort to produce the carbon markets that exist today. One of the classic readings in this area is the work by Peter Levin and Wendy Espeland (2002) who use this sociological approach to examine the role of commensuration in the social construction of commodity. In their chapter titled, "Pollution Futures: Commensuration Commodification and the Market for Air," they focus on how prices become attached to air pollution. Levin and Espeland (2002, 121) argue that "[p]rices, as an expression of value, depend on transforming emissions into comparable, standardized commodities; doing so, in turn, depends on our being able to conceive of the environment as composed of discrete, measurable objects. . . . Commensurative practices are fundamental for making markets."

The most prolific work in this area, however, is that of Donald MacKenzie (2009). In his article, "Making Things the Same: Gases, Emission Rights and the Politics of Carbon Markets," he analyzes the development of emissions permits used in carbon markets and the social process needed to standardize and commoditize the various gases used in these markets. A key finding of his work is that carbon "accountants" have struggled to standardize emissions rights. He calls for efforts to develop better carbon market designs in a struggle to create more effective tools of abatement. A key point of this research is to answer such calls.

The second body of work of relevance to this research is often referred to as the "Varieties of Carbon Governance" approach. The popularity of research in this area has also evolved dramatically with the rise of carbon markets worldwide. A testament to this is the 2009 special issue of *The Journal of Environment & Development*, which explores various facets and case studies focused on the governance of carbon mitigation and the international system that has evolved along with it. Peter Newell (2009) provides an overview of the special edition, including a series of themes critical to understanding the governance of clean development. Such themes include who defines how carbon is governed, conflicts over the CDM policy design and management and a variety of issues relating to power and development.

Other relevant works from this special edition include a piece by Lars Friberg (2009) on the CDM in Brazil, which serves to challenge the common notion that Brazil should be considered a successful case under this policy program. Gudrun Benecke (2009) also explores the success of the CDM in India. He argues that although the program has been functional in India, questions of equity and sustainable justice come into question in this case. Also in this special edition, Miriam Schroeder (2009) examines the patterns of Chinese carbon governance. As the leading CDM host country worldwide, Schroeder argues that the Chinese government is able to use the CDM for its own domestic priorities by adding specific national requirements. This produces a pattern of state-regulated carbon governance, which is unique from any other case.

The most relevant article of the special edition is the work by Harald Fuhr and Markus Lederer (2009) who provide a comparative analysis of carbon governance approaches in recently industrialized states. Despite the expectation that a similar outcome would result from an international policy developed by Western states, just the opposite has occurred. The authors analyze the dominant domestic actors and their responses to find a broad variance among them in each state. From these findings, they conclude that a good understanding of environmental governance patterns is still lacking in developing and emerging economies.

A closely related and even overlapping topic, which is also relevant to this research, is the work on how capitalism impacts environmental outcomes. The main question surrounding this growing debate is how the various capitalist types affect the relative ability of states to address the many facets of climate change. Although my research looks at CDM uptake in emerging economies, most of the work in this area focuses on the developed states. The more recent work reviewed above by Friberg (2009), Fuhr and Lederer (2009) and Schroeder (2009) being the only exceptions to this pattern.

Despite this, there are several innovative ways to approach this issue that have helped to invigorate debate in this area. Engels et al (2008) for instance, uses survey data to trace the behavior of four European countries through the early implementation stages of the European Emissions Trading Scheme (EU ETS)—one of the largest carbon markets in the world today. The goal of this research is to identify patterns of institutional preparation and trading behavior to identify if the varieties of capitalism in these states account for the differences in company trading behavior. The authors argue that because CMEs adopt a strategy that is oriented towards compliance only, the institutional setting produced by these states are not conducive for emissions trading and related market mechanisms. On the other hand, LMEs were found to have more active trading behavior and were focused on generating additional revenue. As a consequence, LMEs promoted a more beneficial institutional setting for emission trading among these advanced industrialized states.

Similar work by John Mikler (2011) focuses on how social attitudes towards the environment may be produced and even perpetuated by the VoCs that shape the domestic institutional environment. As Mikler (2011, 334) describes it, "[t]he effect of environmental concern is not simply related to its magnitude, but the institutional basis for its transmission. This is because social concern may change quite dramatically, but the national institutional contexts of capitalist relations of production tend to endure and frame the context for such concern." Mikler's work focuses on the advanced industrialized states of the US, Germany and Japan. His findings suggest that CMEs tend to produce better environmental outcomes due to the way that complementary institutions function in these states.

In a more recent piece by Mikler and Harrison (2012), Mikler's thesis on how VoCs influence environmental outcomes is extended further. In this case, the authors argue that the relative styles and strengths of technological innovation associated with the main capitalist types may affect their ability to reduce carbon emissions. This work compares practices in the US, Germany and Japan and concludes that because LMEs are more oriented to shareholders, this impairs their ability to address the issue of climate change. In contrast, CMEs may only have incremental technology improvements, but the context of standards setting over market forces allows firms in these states to gradually accumulate the technological knowledge and know-how necessary to adapt.

This review of debates and critiques has helped to illustrate several related facets of this research framework. That is, that the climate change policies of various countries differ from each other, but this variation appears to be a reflection of how political and economic power is organized there. An important contribution of this research is to explore these arguments further as they pertain to environmental markets in emerging economies. Despite the various critiques of the VoC approach presented in this chapter, the comparative capitalism framework remains a useful starting point for understanding these issues within the EMEs. More importantly, with the advances in computing and access to data on EMEs, the VoC framework provides a useful starting point for understanding the variation we find in environmental outcomes—such as CDM participation in a medium n set of cases.

D. CONTRIBUTIONS OF THIS RESEARCH

As the VoC approach has grown in popularity, it has become an increasingly powerful way to understand how the various institutions of advanced industrialized economies influence important outcomes—especially those related to growth and competitiveness. The main contribution of the literature on comparative capitalism has been to establish a framework to help establish the different ways in which firms and countries compete. Although there remains much disagreement about the relative merits of different forms of capitalism, efforts in this area have arguably done more than any other discipline to provide an evidential basis for judgments about the effects of different capitalist forms and to debunk many of the myths of a "one best form" of capitalism. And whereas efforts in this area have been fruitful, the literature on the VoC has also spawned a growing number of criticisms, which I aim to address in my research.

The most important contribution of this research has been to extend the VoC model to a broad range of emerging economies from all regions of the world. Until now, research on development and comparative capitalism has been unable to capture and explain the success of emerging economies in full detail. Whereas development studies have not analyzed the institutional configurations of economic systems in these states, research on comparative capitalism has focused mainly on developed countries within the OECD. To address this issue, my research compares the varieties of capitalism among thirty-one EMEs from every region of the world. An empirical analysis of the institutional configurations of emerging economies is a promising way to enhance the scope of the VoC approach. It may also contribute to research on economic development. Most importantly, emerging economies may present novel varieties of capitalism that have yet to be explored in full detail (Shaw, Cooper & Antkiewiczb 2007). Furthering this understanding is a major goal of my research.

Another contribution of my research is to address the lack of consistent empirical measurement, generalization, and definition found in the literature on comparative capitalism. For largely practical reasons, the VoC approach is more generally concerned with the qualitative understanding of how different kinds of economies function than with developing formal models as in neo-classical economics. This results because the idea of institutional complementarities is non-linear[2] and therefore difficult to test using standard quantitative methods. In other words, because improvements or inefficiencies in one institutional sphere have effects in others—in accordance with the theory of institutional complementary described above—empirical research that uses linear probability cannot adequately account for associations in this model.

One solution to this problem is to use advanced quantitative methods with interactions terms. To do so, the researcher must first acquire these advanced skills and also have done prior research to help establish where theoretically appropriate thresholds might be. In most cases, the basic information for a large enough sample is unavailable or would require extensive research to produce it. Consequently, quantitative approaches in the field often characterize states based on only one or two economic spheres. This requires the unrealistic assumption that one or two sets of economic institutions are sufficient to make generalizations about the entire economy. Unfortunately, this may lead to incorrect findings as predicted by the fallacy of composition: *what is true of the parts is not always true of the whole*. As a consequence, research that is able to map the true interactions of complementary institutions is rare in this literature.

In reflection of this, the main preoccupation of the literature has not been the empirical measurement of national economic competitiveness, but rather the analysis of the inter-relations between economic institutions that support particular strategies for economic competition. This has most often been done using case studies, historical analysis or paired comparisons. The result has been a lack of consistent empirical measurement, generalization and definition. The most important consequence of this factor is that it is difficult to empirically test for superior institutional forms within these models (Amable 2003).

Due to the lack of consistent empirical measurement, generalization, and definition, cross-case comparison has also been impaired. As a consequence, wide scale comparison in the literature is very limited. Until very recently, comparative studies have been conducted in only a handful of cases (Whitley 1999; Wong 2006; Andriesse 2006, 2008; Noble 2005; Orru, et al 1997), and many of the world's emerging economies, outside of China, are rarely included at all. This impedes greater generalization and limits time-series studies as well.

An important contribution of my research has been to address many of the problems related to measurement and empirics that continue to impede the VoC approach. My efforts here are threefold. First, by establishing a set of indicators to measure the complex concepts embedded in this theory, and then extending the VoC research protocol to a set of thirty-one emerging market economies, I hope to begin to establish a baseline for future efforts in this area.

Second, my research design incorporates an innovative research method called Qualitative Comparative Analysis (QCA) to help address the issue of non-linearity. QCA is an analytic technique that uses logic to derive the various pathways to a common outcome. In using this method, I aim to foster a greater understanding of how complex socio-political and ecological systems interact.

Lastly, I also compare the QCA findings to a standard quantitative method. By comparing the findings of this method with a more conventional statistical procedure, I hope to highlight important benefits of QCA that may prove fruitful for furthering our understanding of institutional complementarities and how the various types of capitalism work. My goal here is to shed light on how innovative methodological approaches can be used to improve research in this area, thus addressing this weakness in the literature.

One final criticism of the VoC approach that I address in my research is the focus on within case variance. Critics of the approach argue that the focus on firm and state-level analysis ignores the variance within states and across sectors of the economy. For instance, Bruno Amable (2003) argues that homogeneity within states is questionable. "One may object that business practices, patterns of firms' organization, and even sometimes the regulatory environment differ between the regions of a given country" (Amable 2003, 13). Similarly, others have argued that different economic sectors deploy a variety of competitiveness strategies, making them difficult to compare at the national level. According to Green et al (2010, 29), "the analytical strategy in most of the varieties of capitalism literature is to look at the competitiveness strategies in the dominant economic sectors and to generalize from them to the national level, looking at how national institutions and policies support these." Consequently, few accounts are able to analyze all sectors or industrial clusters in their considerable variety and those that do, suffer from a loss of parsimony.

An important contribution of my research has been to develop a comprehensive and purposive approach for defining the dependent variable that takes this critique into consideration. In defining my outcome variable, I have created a three-part matrix. As described in greater detail later in this book, this matrix seeks to account for economic activity across twenty-three sectors or industries of the economies I study. By using a cluster-based analysis among industries, I am able to take account of how the different economic sectors deploy a variety of competitiveness strategies in a reasonably parsimonious manner.

Despite some flaws, the VoC approach is a promising area of research that is particularly in need of empirically driven data analysis. Considering the impact of economic policies at the macro level, research in this area requires evidence based on reliable data and empirics that can be scientifically tested, reproduced and adapted to improve outcomes. To do so, scholars in the field must move beyond theory to begin to measure and test hypotheses so that they can be applied safely and productively to the real-life issues that we face today.

As this review has helped to illustrate, the research design and goals of this book have purposely been forged to address a broad range of critical holes in this important body of literature. In doing so, my research makes important contributions that help to strengthen and understand the VoC model. By mapping market performance in emerging economies (e.g. successful creation of CDM markets) to the diversity of capitalist types, this research helps to contribute to the debate on institutional influences on market behavior across a wide range of countries and economic types.

My research also provides an essential empirical starting point for understanding the varieties of capitalism found among the EMEs, which should help to improve empirical classification and aid in concept building and theory development. Comparative studies of market structures in emerging economies are sparse, even as these states continue to play an increasing role in the world economy. Not only are these states the future drivers of markets and policies, but they are also essential to the solutions for a broad range of issues at the international level. As such, they deserve further research.

NOTES

1. For further examples of the institutional subsystems (e.g. industrial relations, training systems, corporate governance or inter-firm relations) across countries, see Vitols (2001); Thelen (2001); Pontusson (2005); Estevez-Abe et al (2001); Jackson and Vitols (2001).
2. For a further review of non-linearity, see Benney (2011) or Young (2012)

4 Measuring Environmental Outcomes of Capitalism

Throughout history, political economists have thought long and hard about how to govern the national and international economic architecture. Not surprisingly, economists remain central to the debate over the virtues of market-based approaches to environmental protection. Almost a hundred years ago, the English economist Arthur Cecil Pigou (1920) first suggested that taxes could be used to prevent harms to the environment. Central to his work was the concept of an externality—a cost or benefit that affects a party who did not choose to incur it. In industrial relations, the costs associated with externalities are not born by the producers, and the surrounding community generally suffers for it. As a consequence, the social costs exceed the private costs paid by the firm. To correct these negative externalities, a corrective tax—referred to as a Pigovian tax—was suggested by Pigou.

By the 1960s, economist J.H. Dales (1968) began to write about the incompatibility between markets and common goods. What Dales and others came to understand was that many common pool resources are susceptible to overuse because property rights and political freedoms rationally drive individuals to consume as much as they can, and pay as little as possible for it. To address this, Dales (1968) showed how transferable property rights could be used to protect common goods at an overall lower cost than conventional techniques.

Since the two foundational concepts of corrective taxes and transferable property rights were first theorized, research in this area has grown dramatically. By the 1980s, economists have increasingly encouraged the use of market-based policy instruments such as emissions trading[1] to address environmental problems instead of prescriptive "command and control regulations" that are considered "excessively rigid, insensitive to geographical and technological differences, and inefficient" (Pulver 2013). In reflection of this, the use of market-based governance solutions has become increasingly common as a means to resolve important problems.[2]

To better understand this policy option, this chapter explores how various sets of economic institutions perform in market-based policies used to incentivize new market formation. Understanding these sets of economic institutions can help to explain why a particular outcome results. To illustrate the conceptual framework of this book, I begin with an overview of the Clean Development Mechanism (CDM), which provides a useful case for measuring environmental outcomes within the Emerging Market Economies (EMEs). This chapter also explores how modern capitalism is conceptualized and operationalized in the literature and for this research. It concludes with a brief discussion on the data sources and types used in this research.

A. THE CLEAN DEVELOPMENT MECHANISM (CDM)

Because markets are notorious for overusing common goods, using them to address important policy concerns causes some debate. However, there is reason to be optimistic. Market-based mechanisms, like those that established the sulfur dioxide and nitrous oxide emissions markets in the US and European Union (EU) in the 1990s, have set a well-known precedent for achieving positive outcomes. The goal in this case was to reduce acid rain related emissions levels to fifty percent below 1980 levels. The policies far outreached their goals in the end. In twelve years, the US had reduced their emissions by sixty-five percent, while the EU achieved a seventy percent reduction (U.S. Environmental Protection Agency 2009). The advantage of using markets in this case was that they could be designed to limit emissions by internalizing the cost of pollution into the production process. As the acid rain case illustrates, not only do emissions markets have the potential to achieve large-scale results in a relatively quick time frame, they are expected to do so at a reasonable, although not modest, cost.

A more recent example of market-based policies was implemented as part of the 1997 Kyoto Protocol to the 1992 United Nations Framework Convention on Climate Change (UNFCCC). The UNFCCC is an international environmental treaty produced at the United Nations Conference on Environment and Development (UNCED), held in Rio de Janeiro from June 3–14, 1992. The objective of the treaty is to stabilize greenhouse gas (GHG) concentrations in the atmosphere at a level that would prevent dangerous anthropogenic interference with the climate system. To address its goals, the Kyoto framework required signatories to the treaty to limit or reduce their GHG emissions. By setting such targets, a price mechanism was introduced and the pursuit of emission reductions took on an economic value.

To help advanced countries meet their emission targets, and to encourage the developing countries to contribute to the GHG reduction efforts, negotiators of the Protocol established a global market for emissions reductions through a market based mechanism called the Clean Development Mechanism (CDM). The CDM is a market-based trading mechanism established under Article 12 of the Kyoto Protocol and adopted by the Third Conference of the Parties (COP) to the Framework Convention on Climate Change on December 11, 1997. However, the policy was not fully implemented until

January 2005.[3] The dual goals of the CDM are to promote sustainable development in emerging economies and to allow industrialized countries to earn emissions credits from their investments in emissions-reducing projects in developing countries. Accordingly, the CDM has become an important component of how EU countries intend to comply with their assigned emissions targets because it reduces the cost of compliance.

Unlike the earlier emissions markets in the US and EU, the CDM is not a cap and trade system.[4] The states that are eligible to participate in the CDM are considered non-Annex I countries and therefore have no binding emissions target. Instead, the CDM works like a subsidy to incentivize foreign investors and emerging market firms alike to make clean investments that reduce carbon emissions throughout the developing world. And as Dales suggested back in 1968, by undertaking the project in the developing world, the cost of the pollution reduction occurs where it is most cost effective. This encourages sustainable development and offsets the cost of reducing future emissions, thereby causing developing countries to emit fewer GHGs than they would have otherwise.

Together with the other market mechanisms designed under the Kyoto Protocol, the CDM represents the first global-scale attempt at a market-based solution for addressing the problem of global warming. However, the absence of a "cap" in part of the global emissions trading system necessitates a far more complex design than had been attempted for previous emission markets. Instead of limiting emissions, for example, the CDM is designed as a project-based system that allows non Annex-I countries to earn credits that can then be bought and sold on the global carbon markets.

To date, over 10,974 CDM projects have been submitted to the UNFCCC for review (UNEP/Risø, 2013). Firm investments generating CDM credits vary from sector to sector and reflect both investment in new green technology (e.g. solar power plants) and efficiency improvements in existing industrial processes (e.g. waste heat recovery). The funding for such projects may be sourced domestically or provided from abroad. To earn credits under the CDM, the project must be approved and later verified to confirm that the GHG emissions reductions are real, measurable and additional to what would have occurred in the absence of the project (Pulver 2011). The emissions credits generated are then sold on global emissions markets to allow signatories to the Protocol to meet their legally binding, emissions reduction goals.

The process of applying for a CDM project is very complex and highly monitored, but at times, unevenly regulated. To apply for a CDM project, first a project developer is identified. The project developer is usually comprised of the emerging country firm and a consultant who specializes in CDM projects. The project developer may also include additional third parties such as foreign governments, environmental nongovernmental organizations, or enterprises interested in receiving a share of the carbon credits for use within the firm or for trading purposes.

The project developer draws up a Project Design Document (PDD). The PDD includes information regarding environmental impact, the methodology for calculating the emissions, and an emissions reduction baseline. The PDD also explains how the project will be implemented and monitored as well as what makes the project additional. The notion of additionality is an important feature of the CDM. This requires the initiating firm to prove that the investment would not have taken place without the incentive provided by the CDM. For many firms, this means they take on additional risk (e.g. through a costlier investment or a lesser known but greener technology option). Once a new technology becomes "business as usual" it is no longer eligible for CDM credits.

Next, the PDD is submitted for "Host Country Approval." Each state that is eligible to participate in the CDM establishes a home office that is trained and supervised by the UNFCCC—the UN agency that oversees the CDM process. The domestic or "Host Country" office reviews proposed projects and provides guidance to project developers. Once the project is approved, a "Validator," or a third-party consulting firm that has been trained and certified under the UNFCCC program, reviews the PDD. Once the PDD has been validated and certified as accurate and complete, the entire package is sent to the UNFCCC Executive Board for review. The project is then scrutinized and compared with other global CDM projects. If approved, the project is registered and permission is granted to proceed.

Following a project implementation and monitoring period ranging from three months to a year, the project must then be verified to assure it has been properly managed and implemented. Again, an independent party visits the project site to view the project, verify that it has been completed properly, and to assess the actual emissions reductions. If there are any issues at this stage, all the carbon credit benefits may be lost. This helps to prevent fraud and to prove that the project has been undertaken according to specification.

Once verified, the project is certified and the issuance of Carbon Emission Reduction (CERs) credits finally begins. A CER, often referred to as a "carbon credit," is the unit of credit issued by the CDM Executive Board for emission reductions achieved under the rules of the CDM. The CERs may be used by the project developers to offset their emission targets in the home company or their subsidiaries. They may also be traded and sold in global carbon markets for a profit.

According to a publication by the CDM Executive Board (2011, 72), "Since it was implemented in 2005, the CDM market alone has helped to reduce carbon emissions by a billion tons, attracted $215 billion of green investments to developing countries (more than any private environmental fund) and cut the cost of climate-change mitigation by $3.6 billion USD." Despite this, the success of the CDM market has been quite varied. And as the global economic downturn in 2008 made clear, misadventures in markets can have a massive effect on the global economy. Building a better understanding of how to support such markets will be required as their use gains popularity. The challenge to policy makers, then, is to improve the design and implementation of market-based policies, or to determine once and for all that such efforts are not useful at the international level.

B. MEASURING ENVIRONMENTAL OUTCOMES USING THE CDM

Because the dependent variable in this research is successful and unsuccessful CDM market formation, defining this criterion is an important issue. However, what constitutes this outcome is highly debatable. There are several ways the CDM can be measured and defined.[5] Michael Wara (2010), for example, argues that size matters. Smaller CDM projects indicate a greater dispersion of the policy throughout the economy, which suggests the program was successful. Other research focuses on the social goals, defining success by the extent of increased social and developmental outcomes measured as technology transfer, sustainable development and local capacity building (Gillenwater and Seres 2011). While this approach is parsimonious, a meaningful comparison between states at varying levels of development makes these approaches less than optimal.

One compelling approach measures states by their levels of GHG abatement potential. Enkvist, Dinkel and Lin (2010), authors of the McKinsey and Company's *Global GHG Abatement Cost Curve Report*, point out that states with the highest GHG abatement potential come at the lowest costs to investors. This highly precise approach, however, is costly and time consuming because the science for constructing cost-abatement curves is propriety and still being developed. This makes the data expensive, incomplete, and somewhat unreliable, even if it were accessible to researchers.

Although alternative metrics do exist, there is currently little consensus as to the best approach, and they all require tradeoffs. An important contribution of my research has been to develop a valid and reliable way to assess the CDM program. In doing so, I am able to directly address many of the critiques of the VoC literature and clearly focus on the firm as the unit of analysis.

To do so, I use a firm-centered matrix that considers three means of measurement for the dependent variable. All outcomes are based on projects produced and counted at the firm level. The first of the three measures considers a country's CDM project registration rate. As illustrated in Table 4.1, this variable looks at the total number of registered and unregistered projects in the CDM pipeline as a way to measure the total project success rate for each country. This is found by calculating the number of registered projects and dividing by the total number of submitted projects.

The second scenario of the matrix looks at sector diversity. As illustrated in Table 4.2, this measures the diffusion of the CDM across various sectors or industries in the economy. According to Dechezlepretre et al (2008), a potentially important factor is the variety of CDM projects within a

Table 4.1 Successful Registration Rates

Country	Projects in Validation	%	Rejected. terminated or failed	%	Registration Requested	%	Total Unregistered Projects	%	Registered Projects	Registration Success Rate	Total Projects Attempted
Argentina	20	32%	15	24%	0	0%	35	56%	27	44%	62
Bahrain	0	-----	0	-----	0	-----	0	-----	0	0%	0
Bangladesh	2	29%	2	29%	0	0%	4	57%	3	43%	7
Botswana	0	-----	0	-----	0	-----	0	-----	0	0%	0
Brazil	186	29%	262	41%	2	0%	450	70%	196	30%	646
Chile	38	32%	29	24%	0	0%	67	56%	52	44%	rB
China	1225	31%	796	20%	65	2%	2086	53%	1837	47%	3923
Colombia	40	39%	25	24%	1	1%	66	64%	37	36%	103
Cyprus	1	8%	3	25%	0	0%	4	33%	8	67%	12
Egypt	5	25%	5	25%	0	0%	10	50%	10	50%	20
India	984	38%	787	31%	12	0%	1783	69%	792	31%	2575
Indonesia	71	34%	61	29%	2	1%	134	64%	74	36%	208
Jordan	0	0%	3	50%	0	0%	3	50%	3	50%	6
Kenya	16	59%	4	15%	0	0%	20	74%	7	26%	27
Macedonia	5	56%	3	33%	0	0%	8	89%	1	11%	9
Malaysia	49	21%	80	34%	0	0%	129	55%	106	45%	235
Mauritius	1	33%	1	33%	0	0%	2	67%	1	33%	3
Mexico	56	20%	82	30%	3	1%	141	51%	134	49%	275
Morocco	9	41%	5	23%	0	0%	14	64%	8	36%	22
Niger-ia	7	58%	0	0%	0	0%	7	58%	5	42%	12

Pakistan	23	53%	7	16%	1	2%	31	72%	12	28%	43
Peru	26	40%	11	17%	1	2%	38	58%	27	42%	65
Phil ippines	28	23%	35	29%	1	1%	64	53%	56	47%	120
Qatar	1	50%	0	0%	0	0%	1	50%	1	50%	2
Serbia	5	45%	2	18%	0	0%	7	64%	4	36%	11
Africa	42	58%	15	21%	0	0%	57	78%	16	22%	73
Sri lanka	15	38%	18	45%	0	0%	33	83%	7	18%	40
Thailand	95	41%	67	29%	2	1%	164	71%	66	29%	230
Tunisia	3	60%	0	0%	0	0%	3	60%	2	40%	5
UAE	9	39%	9	39%	0	0%	18	78%	5	22%	23
Vietnam	117	43%	40	15%	4	1%	161	60%	108	40%	269

Table 4.2 Projects and Credits by Sector

Country	Affor	Bio	CO_2	Cem	Coal	Energy Efficiency (EE) House	EE Ind	EE own gen	EE Ser	EE supply side	Energy	Fossil	Fug	Geo
Argentina		5					1	2		1				
Bahrain														
Bangladesh							1							
Botswana														
Brazil		46	1					2			1	6	2	
Chile	2	10								1		1		
China		58		5	55	4		144		2	5	25	1	1
Colombia		2	1									1		
Cyprus														
Egypt		1						1		1		2		
India	1	197		13		20	51	61	2	15		13	3	
Indonesia		11		1			2			2		3	1	4
Jordan												2		
Kenya		1												2
Macedonia												1		
Malaysia		30					3			1		1		
Mauritius														
Mexico		3					3						1	
Morocco		1												
Nigeria						1							3	
Pakistan		1						4		3				
Peru		1								1		2		
Philippines		5						2						1
Qatar													1	
Serbia													1	
South Africa		2				1	1					3	1	
Sri Lanka		1											1	
Thailand		10						3						
Tunisia														
UAE							1			1				
Vietnam		2											1	

Hydro	Landfill	Methane	PFCs and SF6	Reforest	Solar	Trans	Wind	Total Reg Proj	Total Sectors	CERS by 2012
1	10	4	1	1			1	27	10	21,409
								0	0	0
	2							3	2	1,189
								0	0	0
48	30	52	2	2			4	196	12	104,562
15	12	7					4	52	8	27,033
811	50	29	1	3	23	2	618	1837	18	796,053
10	12	3		4		3	1	37	9	13,581
		3					5	8	2	852
	1						4	10	6	7,874
91	13	18	1	6	10	4	273	792	18	190,127
6	7	35	1		1			74	12	27,382
	1							3	2	2,354
1				2			1	7	5	1,481
								1	1	168
2	6	63						106	7	25,428
							1	1	1	0
3	17	94				2	11	134	8	38,138
	1				1		5	8	4	2,526
	1							5	3	17,396
2	1	1						12	6	1,902
18	3	1		1				27	7	9,551
5	5	37					1	56	7	7,664
								1	1	13,748
							3	4	2	1,120
1	5	2						16	8	6,966
5								7	3	1,223
	5	46			2			66	5	13,149
	2							2	1	4,125
	1				2			5	4	825
87	3	13		1			1	108	7	16,402

country. If variety is limited, the CDM is seen as less successful across the entire economy. For example, Mexico has many CDM projects, but in just two areas or sectors. Some suggest this is a sign of weakness in the quality of the markets being produced.

The third scenario looks at total CERs normalized by real GDP to control for the size of the economy. Here, success is defined initially by measuring the number of CERs issued for registered CDM projects per country by December 2012. This takes into account the size of the CDM projects being produced, but then scales the outcome to reflect the size of the individual economy of the country. However, an important caveat must be noted that reflects a vital nuance in the operation of all types of emissions markets.

A carbon market is a commodity market not only for carbon dioxide emissions, but also for other GHGs. For example, there are six GHGs traded in the European Union Emissions Trading Scheme (EU ETS) including: Carbon dioxide (CO_2), Methane (CH4), Nitrous oxide (N_20), Hydro fluorocarbons (HFCs), Perfluorocarbons (PFCs), and Sulphur hexafluoride (SF6). To simplify trading, each gas is commoditized and converted into its tons of carbon dioxide equivalent (tCO_2e). Commoditization essentially translates all the various GHGs into a standard unit and carbon dioxide serves as the unit of account for calculation purposes.

However, there is a problem. As global carbon markets have matured, it has become well understood that two gases in particular have come to present an analytical problem because they are simply not equivalent to other types of commoditized gases. These gases are HFC and N_20. As Table 4.3 illustrates, emissions of both HFC and N_20 gases are considered low hanging fruit because their carbon dioxide equivalents are exponential relative to other gases. As the comparison in Table 4.3 makes clear, by 2012, twenty-two HFC projects accounted for 17% of worldwide CER credits. In contrast, 1,498 hydroelectric power projects are required to produce a similar amount of emissions reductions. Out of over 10,000 projects, less than 100 HFC and N_20 clean development projects account for over 25% of all CERs produced within the CDM.

As a result of this distortion, the European Commission is currently considering a proposal to scale back or eliminate HFC and N_20 payments because they are using up resources that could reduce emissions elsewhere.

Table 4.3 Top Four CER Producing Sectors: HFCs, N_20, Hydro and Wind

Project Type	Total Projects	% Total Projects	2012 CERs	% of Total CERs
HFC	22	0.4%	476,516	17%
Hydroelectric	1,516	27%	472,204	17%
Wind	1,092	19%	305,250	11%
N_20	73	1%	253,563	9%

Likewise, in August 2011, the CDM Executive Board "put a hold on issuing carbon credits for HFC reductions, pending an internal review" (Tollefson 2010, 2). The general goal is to create a new protocol and market for these two gases alone in order to spread the market gains in carbon markets more broadly. Consequently, all HFC and N_20 projects associated with the countries in my sample will be removed from my analysis.

As shown in Table 4.4—the third matrix of success in my study, which considers the final CERs issued for registered CDM projects per country by December 2011—does not include HFC and N_20 projects. Then, to improve comparability, the number of CERs generated per country are normalized or scaled to a uniform measure based on the size of the economy generating it. Normalization refers to the division of a dataset by a common variable in order to negate that variable's effect on the data. This allows underlying characteristics of the data sets to be compared based on the relative size of the economy. In this case, average real gross domestic product (GDP) will be used to normalize the cases. Real GDP (nominal GDP adjusted for inflation) is chosen as the means to measure the total size of the economies in this project because it measures real output alone, and is not affected by prices or inflation.

The final three-part matrix produced in Table 4.5 includes the following scenarios: registration success rate (registered/submitted projects), sector diversity (market impact across various sectors of the economy) and final CERs (less HFC and N_20 project credits) relative to the size of the economy. There are many means for measuring success and failure of CDM market formation. Using the three-part matrix I have proposed will help to establish a rigorous, replicable and precise protocol to evaluate the dependent variable from several perspectives. Although a unified measure of success and failure is difficult, the approach I propose establishes a firm basis for evaluating the outcomes of the dependent variable in my research.

As the summary in Table 4.5 shows, each of the scenarios is assessed and coded as 1 = Successful or 0 = Unsuccessful to produce an overall, combined rank. To determine these outcomes, cluster analysis is used because it is precise and easily replicable. The final synthesis of this ranking produces an aggregated outcome across all three scenarios. Of the thirty-one cases in this study, six (20%) of the cases are considered successful: Argentina, Brazil, China, Colombia, India and Indonesia. The remaining twenty-five cases are therefore considered unsuccessful, and include the following states: Bahrain, Bangladesh, Botswana, Chile, Cyprus, Egypt, Jordon, Kenya, Macedonia, Malaysia, Mauritius, Mexico, Morocco, Nigeria, Pakistan, Peru, Philippines, Qatar, Serbia, South Africa, Sri Lanka, Thailand, Tunisia, UAE and Vietnam.

This matrix is useful for highlighting three aspects of the dependent variable. First, it illustrates the wide range of variation that results. Second, it shows that the outcomes on the dependent variable cannot be explained by the country's level of development. In fact, all three levels of development

Table 4.4 Normalized CER Credits

1) Country	2) Reg CDM Proj	3) CERS by 2012	4) HFC Proj	5) CERS from HFCs	6) N20 Proj	7) CERS from N2O	8) Final CDM Proj	9) Total CERs	10) Av Real GDP 2006–11 (mil US)	11) CERs /Av Real GDP
Argentina	28	28,878	−1	−7,469	0	0	27	21,409	111,026	0.1928
Bahrain	0	0	0	0	0	0	0	0	12,783	0.0000
Bangladesh	3	1,189	0	0	0	0	3	1,189	48,619	0.0245
Botswana	0	0	0	0	0	0	0	0	3,835	0.0000
Brazil	201	142,083	0	0	−5	−37521	196	104,562	854,654	0.1223
Chile	53	30,736	0	0	−1	−3703	52	27,033	182,937	0.1478
China	1875	1,257,404	−11	−362,784	−27	−98,567	1837	796,053	3,434,236	0.2318
Colombia	39	15,917	0	0	−2	−2,336	37	13,581	202,576	0.0670
Cyprus	8	852	0	0	0	0	8	852	17,643	0.0483
Egypt	11	14,580	0	0	−1	−6,706	10	7,874	53,163	0.1481
India	805	274,474	−8	−78215	−5	−6,132	792	190,127	1,043,881	0.1821
Indonesia	75	27,640	0	0	−1	−258	74	27,382	233,532	0.1173
Jordan	3	2,354	0	0	0	0	3	2,354	13,270	0.1774
Kenya	7	1,481	0	0	0	0	7	1,481	18,399	0.0805
Macedonia	1	168	0	0	0	0	1	168	5,453	0.0308
Malaysia	106	25,428	0	0	0	0	106	25,428	159,516	0.1594
Mauritius	1	0	0	0	0	0	1	0	7,723	0.0000
Mexico	136	53,382	−1	−14010	−1	−1,234	134	38,138	737,798	0.0517
Morocco	8	2,526	0	0	0	0	8	2,526	73,309	0.0345
Nigeria	5	17,396	0	0	0	0	5	17,396	84,120	0.2068
Pakistan	13	6,837	0	0	−1	−4,935	12	1,902	78,676	0.0242

Peru	27	9,551	0	0	0	0	27	9,551	65,520	0.1458
Philippines	57	7,775	0	0	–1	–111	56	7,664	116,413	0.0658
Qatar	1	13,748	0	0	0	0	1	13,748	46,186	0.2977
Serbia	4	1,120	0	0	0	0	4	1,120	19,069	0.0587
So. Africa	20	16,666	0	0	–4	–9,700	16	6,966	239,959	0.0290
Sri Lanka	7	1,223	0	0	0	0	7	1,223	22,412	0.0546
Thailand	67	13,653	0	0	–1	–504	66	13,149	131,032	0.1003
Tunisia	2	4,125	0	0	0	0	2	4,125	18,641	0.2213
UAE	5	825	0	0	0	0	5	825	264,800	0.0031
Vietnam	108	16,402	0	0	0	0	108	16,402	29,072	0.5642

1.Country case
2.Number of registered CDM projects by Dec 2011
3.Projected number of CERs by 2012 from all projects
4.Total number of HFC projects per country
5.Projected number of CERs by 2012 from HFC projects per country
6.Total number of N_2O projects per country
7.Projected number of CERs by 2012 from N_2O projects per country
8.Total projected registered CDM projects minus HFC or N_2O projects
9.Total projected CERs by 2012 minus HFC and N_20 project CERS
10.Average Real GDP 2006–11 (Nominal GDP/DEP Deflator, then scaled to millions)
11.Total Final Projected CERs/Average Real GDP

Table 4.5 Dependent Variable Outcome Matrix

Country	1. Project Success	Project Success Cluster	2. Sector Diversity	Sector Cluster	3. Norm Final CERs	Norm CER Cluster	Full Matrix Outcome
Argentina	43.55%	1	10	1	0.1928	0	1
Bahrain	0.00%	0	0	0	0.0000	0	0
Bangladesh	42.86%	1	2	0	0.0245	0	0
Botswana	0.00%	0	0	0	0.0000	0	0
Brazil	30.34%	0	12	1	0.1223	0	1
Chile	43.70%	1	8	0	0.1478	0	0
China	46.83%	1	18	1	0.2318	1	1
Colombia	35.92%	1	9	1	0.0670	0	1
Cyprus	66.67%	1	2	0	0.0483	0	0
Egypt	50.00%	1	6	0	0.1481	0	0
India	30.76%	0	18	1	0.1821	0	1
Indonesia	35.58%	1	12	1	0.1173	0	1
Jordan	50.00%	1	2	0	0.1774	0	0
Kenya	25.93%	0	5	0	0.0805	0	0
Macedonia	11.11%	0	1	0	0.0308	0	0
Malaysia	45.11%	1	7	0	0.1594	0	0
Mauritius	33.33%	1	1	0	0.0000	0	0
Mexico	48.73%	1	8	0	0.0517	0	0
Morocco	36.36%	1	4	0	0.0345	0	0
Nigeria	41.67%	1	3	0	0.2068	1	0
Pakistan	27.91%	0	6	0	0.0242	0	0
Peru	41.54%	1	7	0	0.1458	0	0
Philippines	46.67%	1	7	0	0.0658	0	0
Qatar	50.00%	1	1	0	0.2977	1	0
Serbia	36.36%	1	2	0	0.0587	0	0
S. Africa	21.92%	0	8	0	0.0290	0	0
Sri Lanka	17.50%	0	3	0	0.0546	0	0
Thailand	28.70%	0	5	0	0.1003	0	0
Tunisia	40.00%	1	1	0	0.2213	1	0
UAE	21.74%	0	4	0	0.0031	0	0
Vietnam	40.15%	1	7	0	0.5642	1	0

have produced successful outcomes. Third, this table illustrates some of the interesting variations that occur between the individual scenarios. For example, China is the only successful case that emerges for all three measures. Also, India and Brazil, which are largely considered models of success for CDM market formation, are found to fail when measured on registration success rates alone. However, this turns out to be the result of being first movers in the market.

Perhaps the biggest surprise in the individual scenarios is the measure for effort based on the size of the economy. This scenario appears to produce an additional set of successful cases. Upon further research, these cases can be explained away as outliers. These include the following states: Nigeria, Qatar, Tunisia and Vietnam.

These anomalies occur for two reasons. First, in the cases of Nigeria, Qatar and Tunisia, huge, large-scale projects within the oil industries have produced distorted payoffs in a minimum number of projects. For example, in my sample, the median number of CERs produced per project is approximately 344 CERs. However, the average CERs per project among these three states is 6,430! In Qatar alone, where only one project has been registered in all these years, that project alone produced 13,748 CERs by December 2012. In contrast, China, a country that has exceeded all measures of success, averages 433 CERs per project.

In other words, Nigeria, Qatar and Tunisia each have a very small number of projects with extremely high returns that essentially skews the data. This is not the recognized intent of the CDM, but rather an example of a major problem inherent in its original design. As previously discussed, distorted projects like those found around HFCs and N_20 have resulted in hefty criticism of the CDM program. Solutions to these problems, such as individual markets for these distortionary GHGs, are still being worked out today.

In a similar manner, Vietnam can also be eliminated as a successful case within the third scenario of this matrix after further historical reflection. Vietnam has 108 CDM projects, but each generally produces a very small number of CERs (approximately 148 CERs by 2012). This success is boosted further by the very small size of Vietnam's economy. These characteristics make it distinct from the other outliers discussed here. So what explains Vietnam's appearance of success in this individual scenario?

After further research, it turns out that the positive outcome found in Vietnam is because it was an early testing ground for the CDM. Vietnam, at the time, had many well-established, aid-related relationships that made access easy for the main Annex I states. Because of this, some of the earliest CDM projects were done by US and EU agencies in Vietnam as a way to demonstrate or test the policy. Often a private firm or consulting company was also included in the project and once it was completed, the private actor, having gained the process knowledge, moved on to more profitable projects elsewhere. Although the CDM was not fully implemented until January 2005, the largest CDM project in Vietnam (producing nearly half of all CERs there) was retroactively implemented back to 2001 and heavily supported through the validation process by the US Agency for International Development (USAID). If this one project is removed on the same grounds as the outliers above, Vietnam is no longer successful under this scenario.

Interestingly, these early projects were very fruitful from a developmental stand point, but once market forces were in full force, price regained relative importance over development benefits. In the end, all four outlying cases do provide some helpful insights, and future policy designs for market mechanism may benefit from improved consideration of such cases.

C. CONCEPTUALIZING CAPITALISM IN EMERGING MARKET ECONOMIES

As previous chapters have illustrated, the debate about how to define capitalism is an ongoing process. Moreover, the vast majority of work in this field has focused on the advanced industrialized economies, and less is understood about what capitalism looks like in the developing world. To provide a systematic look at the VoCs within EMEs, each state will also be measured along the independent variables to produce a classification system of the various types of capitalism. To do so, a structured comparison is needed to identify similarities and dissimilarities regarding the institutional configurations of these economic systems. The independent variables in this research include the five economic variables thought to contribute to institutional variation in capitalistic systems, along with four additional control variables. The additional controls are used to advance the VoC theory and to consider what other noneconomic factors might also play a role in the EMEs. Together, these nine independent variables will be used to categorize the types of capitalism found in this research. The resulting classification system will also be used to determine if new varieties of capitalism exist outside the OECD world and which of these varieties are most successful at supporting market-based policy tools like those used to address climate change.

Variety of Capitalism (VoC) Variables

Conceptually and theoretically, this research aims to employ conceptual innovations drawn from the comparative capitalism and development literatures to help generate hypotheses that more accurately reflect the unique features of capitalism in the emerging economies. Such efforts are required because EMEs may have unique forms of coordination in line with the needs of their respective production systems. My research begins with the five classic VoC variables developed by Hall and Soskice (2001), which include labor and industrial relations, finance, inter-firm relations, education and vocational training and corporate governance. The following is an overview of these variables.

Labor and Industrial Relations: the first VoC variable covers the regulation of relations between employees and employers. Here the problem facing enterprises is how to coordinate bargaining over wages and working conditions with their labor force, the organizations that represent labor and other employers. As one source suggests, "[t]he compromise between labour and capital is the cornerstone for high-wage employment and for competitiveness in high-quality industries" (Green et al 2010, 27). The relationships that firms develop to resolve these problems determine, at least in part, their own competencies and the character of an economy's production regime (e.g. LME versus CME). At stake here are wage and productivity levels that condition the success of the firm, along with varying rates of unemployment and inflation that result from wage setting within the economy as a whole.

The labor market is one of the most important sources of difference among capitalist regimes. A helpful distinction found in the literature is the difference between centralized and decentralized systems. LMEs and CMEs, as expected, tend to have decentralized and centralized approaches to labor respectively. Centralized systems are typified by higher levels of employment protection, higher wage replacement rates for unemployment, institutions for labor participation in management, and collective bargaining institutions that reduce wage inequality across sectors and skill levels. Decentralized systems, on the other hand, have weak to no employment protection, less generous unemployment benefits, few or no institutions for workforce participation, firm-level collective bargaining and individualized labor contracts (Hall and Soskice 2001,21–33).

Finance: perhaps the most important area of coordination in capitalism is the financial sphere because it illustrates how capital is sourced or financed within a country. Also referred to as financial markets (Green et al 2010) or capital markets (Radice 2000), these systems act as intermediaries, mobilizing and channeling private savings into investment in the productive sector.

Within this sphere, economies are usually distinguished in terms of "bank-based" or "capital market-based" financing. In bank-based systems, which are typically associated with more "organized" forms of capitalism (e.g. CMEs), banks act as the middle man. Despite their bureaucratic nature, banks also play an important role in creating stability by balancing savings with loans to help minimize liquidity and investment risks (Deeg 1999, 9). Capital market-based systems, which are usually associated with more liberal forms of capitalism (e.g. LMEs), rely more on a direct transfer from savers to borrowers via securities markets (Edwards and Fischer 1994). Although efficient, capital market-based systems are considered much more volatile in regards to risk.

Inter-firm Relations: the third VoC variable drawn from the work of Hall and Soskice (2001) covers the relationship a firm may form with other enterprises. This might include suppliers, clients, inputs, access to technology resulting in "standard-setting," technology transfer and collaborative research and development. Coordination problems in this sphere come from the sharing of proprietary information and the risk of exploitation in joint ventures.

Usually scholars distinguish whether the inter-firm relations are obligatory or competitive. Obligatory relations are associated with CMEs and characterized by cooperation through industry associations or strategic alliances in research and development. In the past, VoC studies have indicated that competitive relations, generally associated with LMEs, produce firms that are more future oriented and therefore more likely to be focused on high technologies. This deters cooperation because such industries are often proprietary in nature. In contrast, obligatory relations being more cooperative produce firms that tend to focus more on traditional industries—although some exceptions should be expected. Accordingly, the degree of coordination via marketing boards, industry associations or the number of mergers and acquisition are both valid indicators within this institutional sphere (Gingerich and Hall 2004).

Education and Vocational Training: the fourth VoC variable describes the type of education system provided by the government and efforts by enterprises to train their employees. Firms must secure a workforce with suitable skills, whereas workers face the problem of deciding how much to invest and in what skills they should invest. As Hall and Soskice (2001, 7) argue, "The skill sets produced by a country's system of training define the possible production strategies in which companies can specialize." The fortunes of individual firms and workers are turned not only on the outcomes of this coordination problem, but on the skill levels and competitiveness of the overall economy.

The most common assumption is that LMEs focus more on the production of general skills than do CMEs. Whereas the reliance on general skills grants access to labor with developed, portable skills, it diminishes the amount of labor with highly specialized skill sets that workers develop in CMEs (Hall and Soskice 2001, 17).

Corporate Governance: the fifth VoC variable focuses on the methods firms use to govern decision making. Each method leads to some variation in the internal structure of the firm. The solutions devised to secure finance and provide returns to investors affect both the availability of finance for particular types of problems and the terms on which firms can secure funds. In other words, this sphere examines how the internal structure of the firm varies. Areas of structural variation might include corporate management, ownership structures and the relevance of certain shareholders and stakeholders.

Past research in this sphere has focused on which actor sets the regulatory framework within the system. This leads to two disparate categories of concentrated or dispersed ownership structures. In the extant literature, a distinction is made between "concentrated" systems with insider control by management, employees and suppliers, versus those with "dispersed" control by outside shareholders (Maher and Andersson 1999). A similar distinction can be made if ownership is concentrated among large block holders, such as families, banks and corporations, or dispersed among a wide range of shareholders (e.g. institutional investors) (Becht and Roel 1999).

Finally, the role of labor could be an important factor influencing the shape of corporate governance (Roe 2003; Blair and Roe 1999). For instance, codetermination[6] is a labor practice where the employees have a role in management of a company. Co-determination policies and higher levels of organized labor are related to disperse systems of governance, whereas the opposite is common in concentrated systems.

Control Variables

The VoC theory assumes a rationalist approach to economic institutions, but in the spirit of Karl Polanyi (1946) and others, it is important to challenge the latent functionalism of the theory if further inroads are to be made in the field of comparative capitalism. This is my motivation for introducing a set of control variables that can shed light on *what else* might be at play. Whereas the VoC framework provides a useful analytic approach for the comparative analysis of capitalist economies, other possible factors include the role of the state, taxes and spending, welfare programs, the nature of competition (quality vs. price) and social capital. In reflection of this, my research asks if economic decisions about green investments may also be influenced by other "non-price" factors.

For greater specification of the model, this research considers four additional control variables: macroeconomic stability, infrastructure levels, strength of public institutions and population size. During the research process, three additional variables were also considered, but were removed from the model as they either lacked variance or had little influence in the model. These include primary education levels, public health and product-market efficiency. All seven of the control variables considered during the research are drawn from the development literature and were selected because they were both highly compelling and consistently cited in the literature as important priorities for developing states. Together, these variables help to give us further insight into the different priorities that may also play a part in the types of capitalism found among the EMEs. The following is an overview of these variables.

Macroeconomic Stability: the context of stability, whether social or economic, has long been understood to play a role in determining outcomes. For example, macroeconomic stability has long been cited as critical to growth in all economies. The adverse effects of macroeconomic instability create a business environment in which it is difficult to plan or invest. According to the Global Competitiveness Report developed by Michael Porter et al (2006), "[m]ismanagement of public finances and high inflation—one of its frequent by-products, greatly complicates the business environment, undermining incentives for investment based on long-term planning" (xiii). Issues addressed in this area include national savings rates, inflation, price volatility, interest rates, public sector debt and deficits and exchange rate risk.

Infrastructure Levels: there is also a significant body of empirical research that has shown that physical infrastructure (e.g. roads, bridges and ports) are essential for growth and investment to flourish. Good infrastructure is essential for reducing transport time and promoting communication. It is also required for the efficient and equitable distribution of supplies (especially energy supplies) as well as other benefits of growth. A number of empirical studies have found that the different rates of development found in Asia and Africa can be partly traced to the dissimilar infrastructure endowments of the two regions (Porter et al. 2006). And weak infrastructure was also perceived as being an important impediment to private-sector development in much of Latin America. According to Borensztein et al (1998), physical infrastructure can foster productivity, growth and investment. In reflection of its many influences on economic coordination, infrastructure is explored as a control variable in this research.

Public Institutions: another factor found in EMEs that may influence outcomes is the idea of transparency, efficiency and credibility in public institutions. As William Easterly (2006) has noted, the strength of public institutions can have significant implications on growth, productivity and the behavior of economic agents. Countries that are accountable to their domestic populations have a clear advantage in this regard, and outside investors care even more. Issues encompassed in this area include property rights, corruption, judicial independence, regulatory burdens, efficient use of resources and the effect of public safety on the business environment. Understanding the influential role of public institutions seems necessary because in many EMEs, the state plays a crucial role in shaping the economic system.

Population: like many issues faced by developing states, most environmental problems are aggravated by population growth. Today, the world's population has surpassed seven billion people and continues to grow by some seventy-eight million additional people each year (UNFPA 2013). According to the United Nations Population Fund (UNFPA), since the 1950s, the majority of this growth has occured in the cities of less-developed countries, which has profound implications for the development process. "Governments need to be able to gather adequate information about population dynamics and trends in order to create and manage sound policies and generate the political will to appropriately address both current and future needs" (UNFPA 2013).

Not surprisingly, of the four main foci of the UNFPA (2013), the impact of population on climate change in the developing world is their "most pressing" concern. Population issues are critical to understanding climate change and its consequences because recent research shows that population dynamics (variations in age, urbanization and growing income) can add to the complexity of human-related rises in GHGs (Moser and Satterthwaite 2008; Alyanak 2009; Hardee and Jiang 2009). In other words, the relationship between environmental degradation and growth is especially well documented, and the EMEs are at great risk. Understanding this relationship further seems like a necessary pursuit.

D. DATA COLLECTION

The empirical data for this comparative research include both quantitative indicators and survey research data. Since the CDM was first implemented in January 2005, quantitative indicators will be used from year-end 2005. Similarly, survey research data for this study will be sourced from the 2005 Executive Opinion Survey from the World Economic Forum (World Economic Forum 2006). The following section illustrates how the data were collected and treated.

Data Sources

The data for this research are drawn from five well-known and commonly used sources. These include, but are not limited to, the following:

- *The CDM/JI Pipeline Analysis and Database, UNEP Risø Centre (2012)*: The CDM pipeline is an online registry of GHG-reducing CDM projects initiated by firms in developing countries. It is updated and managed by the UNEP Risø Centre to provide clear and accurate data on the capacity development of the CDM.
- *Global Competitiveness Index, World Economic Forum (2006)*: The Global Competitiveness Index (GCI) was developed by Sala-i-Martín and Artadi (2004) of the World Economic Forum to help better understand and benchmark the many factors involved in economic growth. It measures the microeconomic and macroeconomic foundations of national competitiveness.
- *World Development Indicators, World Bank (2012)*: The World Development Indicators are drawn from the World Bank's collection of development indicators, compiled from officially-recognized international sources. It presents the most current and accurate global development data available and includes national, regional, and global estimates.
- *World Economic Outlook Databases, International Monetary Fund (2012)*: The World Economic Outlook data is drawn from the International Monetary Fund's information databases. It provides downloadable time-series data for a wide range of economic indicators.
- *ILOSTAT, International Labor Organization (2012)*: ILOSTAT provides recent data for over 100 indicators in 165 economies. It is the most recent labor database in the world, and since 2008, has been expanded to include and replace the ILO's former database called LABORSTA.

Treatment of the Data

To begin to understand the relevant data, the dependent and independent variables were operationalized to produce a series of measures to assess each economy. As part of this research protocol, an established set of indicators are described in Appendix A. Once the defined data were collected from these sources, they were compiled into an indexed dataset. The proposed index is a dynamic scoring model containing both survey data and quantitative indicators. The index includes sets of subindicators used to measure the five independent and four control variables theorized to represent the economic institutions in EMEs.

The independent and control variable category scores are produced by calculating the unweighted mean of the underlying indicators and scaling the data from 0–7, where 7 = highest/strongest association with the Liberal Market Economy type. The control variables also follow this same pattern, but are not associated with a specific ideal type. Each category is based on two to five underlying subindicator. Every subindicator will contribute equally to its parent category and every category will contribute equally to the overall outcome for each case. In the quantitative portion of this research, the aggregate score will be considered the baseline score for each case.

From the proposed index, a typology of the types of capitalism is developed for the thirty-one cases in this project. To develop this typology, each case will be categorized based on the two main ideal types, as well as any hybrid variations that can be established. Next, the patterns produced from these outcomes will be assessed to see which combinations of independent variables seem to lead to successful and unsuccessful market formation for the CDM.

Instrumentation

The main instrument used in this research is the index described above. This will also be the main resource for the QCA and logistic data analysis in the following chapters. Table 4.6 illustrates the summarized data for the VoC variables found within the index. Here, each of the countries in the sample along with their level of development is listed on the left. Next, the final index value for each of the VoC variables is listed in the subsequent columns. Finally, the grey-scale coding included for each variable illustrates the dichotomized classification for each variable. White coloring indicates a Controlled Market Economy (CME) classification, and grey indicates a Liberal Market Economy (LME) classification.

To illustrate these outcomes, let me focus on the case of Argentina. As illustrated in Table 4.6, the state scored low on the variables for labor, finance, inter-firm relations and corporate governance, but high on the variable for education and vocational training. As will be illustrated in greater detail during the discussion of the VoC typology, this suggests that Argentina is a CME ideal type because it was classified as CME on four out of five VoC characteristics.

A similar summary of the control variables is provided in Table 4.7. These indicators are also scaled and then dichotomized, but do not correlate to a specific ideal type. Instead, the dichotomization here indicates a

Table 4.6 Summary of the VoC Data Instrument

Country	Level of Dev	VOC 1 Labor	VOC 2 Finance	VOC 3 Inter-firm Relations	VOC 4 Ed & Voc Training	VOC 5 Corp Gov
Argentina	3	3.02	2.60	3.34	4.24	3.82
Bahrain	3	4.66	3.96	3.64	3.95	4.42
Bangladesh	3	4.99	2.37	2.88	2.59	5.02
Botswana	3	4.80	3.18	3.34	3.47	3.58
Brazil	1	3.64	2.97	3.99	3.72	4.18
Chile	2	5.19	4.19	4.23	4.57	4.78
China	2	3.91	2.81	3.57	3.51	3.58
Colombia	2	4.27	2.81	3.86	3.94	4.60
Cyprus	3	4.18	3.54	4.28	4.67	4.00
Egypt	2	3.65	2.89	3.67	3.54	3.58
India	2	4.18	4.14	4.50	4.36	4.60
Indonesia	2	4.32	3.63	3.45	3.76	4.18
Jordan	3	5.15	3.84	3.67	4.26	3.58
Kenya	3	4.67	2.99	3.49	3.25	4.18
Macedonia	3	4.16	2.69	3.12	3.69	4.00
Malaysia	1	5.12	4.88	4.75	4.93	6.22
Mauritius	3	4.64	3.52	4.12	3.75	5.62
Mexico	1	4.24	2.70	3.88	3.89	3.40
Morocco	2	3.93	2.73	3.37	3.53	3.58
Nigeria	3	4.94	2.65	3.32	2.82	4.42
Pakistan	2	4.48	3.25	3.73	3.09	4.78
Peru	2	4.27	3.14	3.63	3.60	4.78
Philippines	2	4.10	2.88	3.65	3.95	2.98
Qatar	3	5.27	4.24	3.84	4.43	4.00
Serbia	3	4.71	2.70	3.04	3.57	4.18
So. Africa	1	4.32	4.97	3.99	3.99	5.80
Sri Lanka	3	3.62	3.00	3.46	3.26	4.18
Thailand	1	5.08	3.56	4.02	4.43	4.60
Tunisia	3	4.73	3.46	4.38	4.73	5.68
UAE	2	5.30	4.05	4.26	4.34	3.58
Vietnam	3	4.25	2.62	3.01	3.03	2.20

Note: Lev of Dev = level of EME development: 1 = Advanced Emerging, 2 = Secondary Emerging and 3 = Frontier Emerging

high score, found in grey, or a low score, found in white. Again, in the case of Argentina, the dichotomous outcomes indicate a high score on the variable for macroeconomic stability. However, it receives a low score on the variables for infrastructure, public institutions and population size.

Table 4.7 Summary of the Control Variables

Country	Level of Dev	CON 1 Macro Stability	CON 2 Infrastructure	CON 3 Public Institutions	CON 4 Population
Argentina	3	5.0965	3.3455	2.7629	1.1748
Bahrain	3	6.0939	4.2577	4.0273	1.0033
Bangladesh	3	4.859	2.3091	2.6474	1.6474
Botswana	3	5.5448	3.6082	4.4546	1.0086
Brazil	1	3.7038	3.1534	3.0467	1.8564
Chile	2	6.0383	4.5434	4.611	1.0751
China	2	6.4547	3.7295	3.5503	7.0033
Colombia	2	4.9254	2.8753	3.3306	1.1982
Cyprus	3	5.1463	4.5784	4.6024	1.0048
Egypt	2	3.5778	3.5372	3.9246	1.3417
India	2	4.5667	3.3871	4.3131	6.2496
Indonesia	2	4.7951	2.8105	3.5998	2.0467
Jordan	3	4.2506	4.109	4.6278	1.0249
Kenya	3	4.4807	2.4019	2.8642	1.164
Macedonia	3	5.3501	2.7535	2.8847	1.0094
Malaysia	1	5.4667	5.3372	5.1156	1.1202
Mauritius	3	4.2718	3.983	4.0042	1.0057
Mexico	1	5.0573	3.5512	3.2909	1.4903
Morocco	2	4.6925	3.2966	3.7182	1.14
Nigeria	3	4.8348	2.424	3.1055	1.6439
Pakistan	2	4.5689	3.1523	3.1906	1.7305
Peru	2	4.9966	2.5511	2.8195	1.1269
Philippines	2	4.6206	2.6352	3.0298	1.3939
Qatar	3	6.4126	3.9989	5.1831	1.0038
Serbia	3	4.6093	2.7183	3.2171	1.0343
So. Africa	1	5.1886	4.4474	4.257	1.2173
Sri Lanka	3	4.023	2.8143	3.149	1.0905
Thailand	1	5.4743	4.6846	4.2515	1.3071
Tunisia	3	4.9	4.4	5.1	1.0462
UAE	2	6.187	5.4216	4.9913	1.0187
Vietnam	3	5.3035	2.6099	3.4898	1.3794

Note: Lev of Dev indicates the level of development within the EMEs. 1 = Advanced Emerging, 2 = Secondary Emerging and 3 = Frontier Emerging

Through this established research protocol, the final data will also be analyzed using a mixed-method research design to explain which preexisting economic institutions and in what combinations produce success or failure in creating markets for the CDM. Through this approach, I hope to develop a better understanding of the causal mechanisms of market development in the EMEs.

NOTES

1. "Emissions trading require a cap to effectively reduce emissions, and the cap is a government regulatory mechanism. After a cap has been set by a government political process, individual companies are free to choose how or if they will reduce their emissions. Failure to reduce emissions is often punishable by a further government regulatory mechanism, a fine that increases costs of production. Firms will choose the least-costly way to comply with the pollution regulation, which will lead to reductions where the least expensive solutions exist, while allowing emissions that are more expensive to reduce" (Pulver, forthcoming).
2. Some examples including fishery permits, allocation of water rights and a range of emissions markets (Keohane and Olmstead 2007). For other examples, see Stavins 2001; Butzengeiger-Geyer et al 2011; Sovacool 2011.
3. According to the CDM Pipeline, the first registered CDM project was by a Brazilian company on November 18, 2004. Then beginning in January 2005, numerous countries filed for registration (although some early projects are considered retroactive back as early as 2001)(UNEP/Risø 2013).
4. To establish an emission or "carbon" market, a government or other central authority must first set a limit or "cap" on the amount of emissions. Once the overall allowable level of pollution is determined, market actors are left to optimize the use of emissions rights by allocating resources within those limits. This is done by trading the rights to pollute within the carbon market. Firms that keep their emission levels below their allotted level may sell their surplus permits to other firms or use them to offset excess emissions in other parts of their company. Failure to reduce emissions is often punishable through a fine that increases costs of production. Firms will choose the least costly way to comply with the pollution regulation, which will lead to reductions where the least expensive solutions exist (Stavins 2001).
5. Another way to evaluate the CDM is by normalizing the cases using grid emissions factors (GEF). The GEF is the amount of carbon dioxide emissions associated with the production of each unit of electricity in an electricity grid. However, GEFs tend to be regional and varied, making them difficult to use here.
6. According to Fitzroy and Kraft (2005), the word *codetermination* is a literal translation from the German word *Mitbestimmung*, where co-determination laws began in 1976. Such laws mandate that worker representatives hold seats on the boards of all companies employing over 500 people. Workers in large companies usually form special bodies called work councils, or may be given seats on the board. In smaller companies, they elect worker representatives to act as intermediaries to protect and inform workers about company labor practices.

5 Varieties of Capitalism (VoC) in the Developing World

One of the most enduring questions in the Varieties of Capitalism (VoC) literature is about the convergence and divergence of capitalism. Will the diffusion of capitalism lead to a greater proliferation of capitalist types, or turn capitalism into a unified ideology? Surprisingly, this question has a long history. Since its earliest roots, it was a quest to determine which mode of production was theoretically superior. The question was amplified after World War I and II, and then again in the 1960s at the height of the Cold War. It was reexamined in the 1990s with the fall of communism and today, the same question is asked in the context of globalization. And each time this question is asked, attention is focused on national differences in the institutions and practices of capitalism as an explanation for the resulting variation found in national economic performance. Some researchers even attempt to identify the direction of institutional innovation because the outcomes of these sets of institutions can result in the substantial redistribution of economic and political power.

The aim of the present chapter is to establish a basis for the VoCs in the developing world. In particular, I systematically examine the convergence of capitalist types using the data from this research. I begin by developing a typology of the VoCs in the Emerging Market Economies (EME). From this, several questions emerge. Do the VoC ideal types exist within the EMEs? Do specific types of capitalism produce better outcomes? Is there evidence of convergence or divergence? By assessing such questions empirically, I hope to extend this age-old question to the developing world.

A. TYPOLOGY OF THE VARIETIES OF CAPITALISM IN EMERGING MARKET ECONOMIES

This research, due to its comparative framework, assumes that among institutions, variation is possible, desirable and necessary. Yet because of its embeddedness, the science behind the existing variation is extremely complex and difficult to model. As Hollingsworth et al. (1994, 8) argue, "[t]he object of comparative empirical research on institutional arrangements for coordinating economic activity is to determine the relative importance of the various modes of governance in different contexts, to describe how they are articulated with one another, and to assess the extent and direction of change in regimes over time."

To achieve these objectives and gain further insights into the progress of capitalism among them, my analysis begins by developing a typology of the VoCs found among the thirty-one countries included in my sample. To do so, I follow the previously specified VoC classification system illustrated in Table 5.1. The point is to produce a typology that provides minimum variability within types and a maximum variability between types, but is also sufficient for addressing the questions raised by this research.

As Figure 5.1 indicates, each country case is categorized based on the two main ideal types as well as any hybrid variations that can be established. The types include the Controlled Market Economy (CME), the Liberal Market Economy (LME) and two distinct hybrid types. Figure 5.1 provides a detailed definition for each "type" produced in the typology. To be classified as an LME, a case must score a one on four or more economic institutions. CME types must score a zero on four or more economic institutions. Hybrid cases are those that do not fall into one of the defined pure ideal types (e.g. LME and CME types).

Table 5.1 Protocol for the VoC Ideal Types

VoC Variables	Liberal Market Economy (LME)	Coordinated Market Economy (CME)
Labor Relations	Decentralized Labor	Centralized Labor
Finance	Market-based Financing	Bank-based Financing
Inter-firm Relations	Competitive	Obligatory
Education and Vocational Training	General Skills	Highly Skilled
Corporate Governance	Concentrated Ownership	Dispersed Ownership

CME	4 or more CME categories
CME-Hybrid	Hybrid: 3 CME Categories/2 LME categories
LME-Hybrid	Hybrid: 3 LME Categories/2 CME categories
LME	4 or more LME categories

Figure 5.1 Definition of Types

The patterns produced from these outcomes are then assessed to see what patterns physically exist. Table 5.2 illustrates the resulting typology of VoCs found to exist among the EMEs in my sample. The overall objective of the typology is not to suggest that a set number of ideal types exist, but

Table 5.2 VoC Typology of Ideal Types Found among EMEs

Country	LOD	VoC A	VoC B	VoC C	VoC D	VoC E	DV	Type	Success?
Argentina	3	0	0	0	1	0	1	CME	Yes
Bahrain	3	1	1	0	1	1	0	LME	No
Bangladesh	3	1	0	0	0	1	0	Hybrid	No
Botswana	3	1	0	0	0	0	0	CME	No
Brazil	1	0	0	1	0	0	1	CME	Yes
Chile	2	1	1	1	1	1	0	LME	No
China	2	0	0	0	0	0	1	CME	Yes
Colombia	2	0	0	1	1	1	1	Hybrid	Yes
Cyprus	3	0	0	1	1	0	0	Hybrid	No
Egypt	2	0	0	0	0	0	0	CME	No
India	2	0	1	1	1	1	1	LME	Yes
Indonesia	2	0	1	0	0	0	1	CME	Yes
Jordan	3	1	1	0	1	0	0	Hybrid	No
Kenya	3	1	0	0	0	0	0	CME	No
Macedonia	3	0	0	0	0	0	0	CME	No
Malaysia	1	1	1	1	1	1	0	LME	No
Mauritius	3	1	0	1	0	1	0	Hybrid	No
Mexico	1	0	0	1	1	0	0	Hybrid	No
Morocco	2	0	0	0	0	0	0	CME	No
Nigeria	3	1	0	0	0	1	0	Hybrid	No
Pakistan	2	1	0	0	0	1	0	Hybrid	No
Peru	2	0	0	0	0	1	0	CME	No
Philippines	2	0	0	0	1	0	0	CME	No
Qatar	3	1	1	1	1	0	0	LME	No
Serbia	3	1	0	0	0	0	0	CME	No
So. Africa	1	0	1	1	1	1	0	LME	No
Sri Lanka	3	0	0	0	0	0	0	CME	No
Thailand	1	1	0	1	1	1	0	LME	No
Tunisia	3	1	0	1	1	1	0	LME	No
UAE	2	1	1	1	1	0	0	LME	No
Vietnam	3	0	0	0	0	0	0	CME	No

Note: VoC A = labor relations; VoC B = finance; VoC C = inter-firm relations; VoC E = education and training; VoC E = corporate governance; CME = Controlled Market Economy; LME = Liberal Market Economy; and Hybrid = a hybrid ideal type; Level of Development (LOD): 1 = Advance Emerging, 2 = Secondary Emerging and 3 = Frontier Emerging to establish a baseline to begin to improve our general understanding of the types of capitalism that exist among the EMEs. In this way, I hope to advance the precision of VoC classification among the emerging markets, so further variety within and between their subtypes can be addressed by future scholars.

B. ASSESSING CAPITALIST TYPES—THREE RESEARCH QUESTIONS

Given that various economic institutions have been shown to produce unique types of capitalism, it is reasonable to assume that there are consequences from these types. I test several underlying assumptions in my research, but they can be generalized into three sets of questions. Because the VoC theory has only been tested on industrialized states, my first research question looks at the VoCs found in the developing world. Do the VoC ideal types exist within the EMEs? My second question is focused on how well each variety performs in terms of environmental outcomes. Do specific types of capitalism produce better performance under the Clean Development Mechanism (CDM)? My third question looks at the idea of convergence and divergence in capitalist forms. Is there evidence of convergence or divergence in my sample? Together, these three research questions frame this analysis.

Varieties of Capitalism in Emerging Market Economies

Although the types of capitalism found in the advanced economies are well understood, less is known about the varieties found among the EMEs. Even the process of industrialization for these states has been rather unique. In the first Industrial Revolution, countries generally began to export goods and services successfully to foreign markets, and this allowed their nascent industries to become efficient by creating economies of scale. However, many of the more recent industrializers have mainly consolidated their domestic industries prior to liberalizing or opening their economies to outside markets. Although some exceptions exist,[1] this general pattern explains the rapid success of export sectors in some EMEs.

There are other historical considerations that make these states unique. Many, for example, were former colonies or formerly communist states. And with decolonization in the 1960s, and then the breakdown of the socialist system in the 1990s, the movement towards global capitalism has increased the frequency of EMEs rising from nontraditional states—each with their own unique variety of capitalism. Does this suggest that new forms of capitalism may exist?

Hall and Soskice (2001) originally proposed two main ideal types—Liberal Market Economies (LMEs) and Coordinated Market Economies (CME). However, because some EMEs have followed a new pattern of industrialization, such innovations illustrate how hybrid forms of capitalism may have

Table 5.3 Frequencies of VoC Types

		Frequency	Percent	Valid %	Cumulative Percent
Valid	CME	14	45.2	45.2	45.2
	Hybrid	8	25.8	25.8	71.0
	LME	9	29.0	29.0	100.0
	Total	31	100.0	100.0	

formed. The term *hybrid* is used to describe an instance when an economy is composed of a mix of subsystems from either market (e.g. LMEs) or coordinated (e.g. CME) types. Hybrid cases may also include elements of "state-compensating coordination" where the state itself helps to coordinate the economy to compensate for weaker elements of the operating economic institutions (Hancke, Rhodes and Thatcher 2009).

From this basis, it is reasonable to assume that the two pure VoC ideal types should exist among the EMEs, just as they do in the advanced industrialized states. Moreover, because hybrid types may contain weaker elements within their economic institutions and EMEs are states that are currently performing well, LMEs and CMEs should be more common than hybrid ideal types. Using the typology of VoCs, some basic conclusions can be made.

Based on the resulting frequencies shown in Table 5.3, CMEs and LMEs do make up the majority of cases. There are nine LMEs (29%) and fourteen CMEs (45%). In contrast, there are only eight instances of hybrid types (26%), but twenty-three pure ideal types overall, making up 74% of the total cases. The most important finding here is simply how well the VoC theory seems to hold, especially for the more advanced emerging states.

Market Performance by Type

Markets are the implicitly or explicitly negotiated outcome of a social problem that sets out to define property rights, governance structures, rules of exchange and conceptions of control (Fligstein 2002). However, Hall and Soskice (2001, 37) argue "that the institutional structure of a particular economy provides firms with advantages for engaging in specific types of activities there." The advantage, then, goes to those market actors who are best suited to the economic setting in which they are embedded. Because LMEs primarily coordinate their activities through market relations, they are considered more efficient in market settings. This suggests that market-based types of capitalism will have an advantage with market-based policies like the CDM. However, based on the crosstab of success rates among the VoCs presented in Table 5.4, it was found that both CMEs (29%) and hybrid (12%) cases produce higher rates of success then LMEs (11%).

Table 5.4 Crosstab of Success Rates among VoC Ideal Types

	LME	CME	Pure (LME+CME)	Hybrid	Total
Success	11% (1)	29% (4)	22% (5)	12% (1)	19% (6)
Failure	89% (8)	71% (10)	78% (18)	88% (7)	81% (25)
	100% (9)	100% (14)	100% (23)	100% (8)	100% (31)

Another way to explore the idea of market performance is to consider how pure and hybrid ideal types might vary. For example, Bob Hancke (2009) has noted that some evidence does exist for hybrid ideal types even within OECD states. Although work in this area is only theoretical and has not been empirically tested, Gingerich and Hall (2004) argue that hybrid cases will be less efficient than "purer" types because the economic institutions are misaligned and do not produce efficient institutional complementarities.[2] In contrast, Colin Crouch (2005) has argued that this deficiency in ideal types should not be automatically assumed. If we accept the idea of institutional complementarities, "then it may also be possible, in theory, for mixed economies to find their own forms of coordination in line with the needs of their respective production systems" (Hancke 2009, 282). Hence, the verdict on hybrid-type performance is undecided.

Because it is generally assumed that pure ideal types will more readily adapt to market settings, it seems reasonable to infer that they are also the most plausible types of capitalism to produce a successful market outcome. Because economic institutions found in hybrid types of capitalism are expected to be less efficient in market settings, EMEs that are classified as hybrid types are less likely to produce successful cases of CDM market formation. Despite these expectations, some interesting nuances result.

When only pure and hybrid cases are considered, economies with hybrid or mixed modes of coordination do perform the worst. For example, hybrid cases produce fewer successful cases of CDM market formation compared with cases classified as pure ideal types. As Table 5.4 illustrates, pure ideal types perform better overall (22%) compared to hybrid types (12%), but this is due to the high success rate of CME types in particular. In short, CME types (29%) perform better than hybrid types (12%), but LME types (11%) performed the worst of the three types overall.

My research suggests that the EMEs with the purer types of capitalism produced the best outcomes overall. Hybrid ideal types, as theorized, do appear to produce less efficient institutional complementarities. However, CMEs far outperformed both the LMEs and the hybrid cases. The good news is that for most of the emerging world, CMEs are the most common form of capitalism, with LMEs and hybrid types basically tied for second. This suggests that the type of economy should be taken into greater consideration when designing and implementing market-based policies such as the CDM.

Convergence and Divergence of Capitalism

In the fields of political economy and economic sociology, the story of convergence and divergence generally includes analyzing the efficacy of one model of capitalism compared to another. More importantly, the international world market is seen as a sort of natural lab where various national models of capitalism evolve and compete, "with the successful ones replacing the unsuccessful in a process of institutional change by imposition or adoption" (Radice 2000, 725). However, "the continued viability of any particular institutional order depends not on some intrinsic, suprahistorical superiority, but on its 'goodness of fit' with its environment and its evolutionary adaptability: change then comes about when viability is lost" (Radice 2000, 737). In other words, it is not that one type is better than another, but rather that a new setting or environment develops, and the associated comparative advantage diminishes.

In the contemporary study of capitalism, it is often argued that as a result of globalization, eventually all capitalistic states will converge to one single type. This in turn was expected to produce uniformity of national economic institutions. However, Lauder, et al (2008) have argued that national institutions and each state's system of coordination will respond to the opportunities and challenges posed by economic globalization from the comparative advantage conferred by their "type" of capitalism. Instead of conformity, states that take advantage of their comparative strengths will cause a divergence or variety of capitalist types to emerge.

This debate is not all that different from the literature on democratic types. Nevertheless, it is most useful to compare the process of capitalistic divergence to the principle of comparative advantage (Ricardo 1966). Just as comparative advantage promotes greater variety and output in the terms of trade, so does the pursuit of specialization among types of capitalism increase the varieties of capitalism that exist. And with the diffusion of globalization, states have increasingly been able to benefit from their comparative institutional advantages. As Lauder, Brown and Ashton (2008, 3) and others have argued, "[i]n this way, national characteristics are preserved and, rather than globalization leading to convergence, distinctive national approaches to the global economy ensure continued national divergence."

Although debate in this area is mainly theoretical, what does appear to be clear from the data is that as we move up the levels of development within the EMEs, we do appear to find a consolidation of ideal types. As Table 5.5 illustrates, the most advanced cases in my sample were more likely to be pure ideal types. Cases at the lower end of the ranking are more likely to be hybrid types. In this case, convergence towards pure, and perhaps more functional, forms does appear to be occurring in these states.

If these cases are considered by subgroup, some interesting factors also result. For example, of the five Advanced Emerging economies in my

Table 5.5 Ranked by Level of Development

Country Category	Country	LOD	VoC type
Advanced Emerging Economies	Brazil*	1	CME
	Mexico	1	CME-Hybrid
	Malaysia	1	LME
	So. Africa	1	LME
	Thailand	1	LME
Secondary Emerging Economies	China*	2	CME
	Egypt	2	CME
	Indonesia*	2	CME
	Morocco	2	CME
	Peru	2	CME
	Philippines	2	CME
	Pakistan	2	CME-Hybrid
	Colombia*	2	LME-Hybrid
	Chile	2	LME
	India*	2	LME
	UAE	2	LME
Frontier Emerging Economies	Argentina*	3	CME
	Botswana	3	CME
	Kenya	3	CME
	Macedonia	3	CME
	Serbia	3	CME
	Sri Lanka	3	CME
	Vietnam	3	CME
	Bangladesh	3	CME-Hybrid
	Cyprus	3	CME-Hybrid
	Nigeria	3	CME-Hybrid
	Jordan	3	LME-Hybrid
	Mauritius	3	LME-Hybrid
	Bahrain	3	LME
	Qatar	3	LME
	Tunisia	3	LME

* Positive outcome reported on the DV

sample, eighty percent were pure ideal types (three LME and one CME). Unlike the other two subgroups, the Advanced Emerging states are composed of mainly of liberal-market variations, which make up sixty percent of the subgroup.

In the Secondary Emerging economies, there are eleven cases. In contrast to the Advanced Emerging economies, the Secondary Emerging economies are composed of sixty-four percent controlled-market variations and thirty-six percent liberal-market variations. Just like the Advanced Emerging states, however, eighty-two percent of this subgroup contains ideal types (three LME and six CME), and only eighteen percent hybrid cases.

The Frontier Emerging subgroup is the largest with fifteen cases in the sample. Like the Secondary Emerging category, the Frontier Emerging category is sixty-seven percent controlled-market variation and thirty-three percent liberal-market variation. Perhaps the most interesting finding here is that this category contains more than 1/3 hybrid types. With only sixty-seven percent pure ideal types (three LME and seven CME), the Frontier Emerging subgroup has about twice as many hybrid types as the other two categories.

The substantial number of hybrid cases in the Frontier Emerging economies does seem to confirm the notion that mixed modes of coordination produce less efficient institutional complementarities. This is further supported by the fact that eighty percent of the successful cases in my sample were pure VoC types. But that still leaves the question, "why?" What other priorities or institutions are at play? What causes these new sources of diversity? These competing priorities and their underlying causes will be explored further in Chapter 6 and 7.

C. CONCLUSIONS ON CAPITALIST CONVERGENCE

Although the types of capitalism in the advanced economies are well understood, less is known about the varieties found among the EMEs. To help establish a basis for the VoCs in the developing world, this chapter has explored not only what the VoCs are like and not like, but also the causal processes behind the emerging patterns. By drawing on the typology developed in this chapter, I empirically explored a set of questions focused on the VoC types, the outcomes they create for policy and, most importantly, if there is evidence for the convergence or divergence of capitalism.

What this research seems to make clear is that, undoubtedly, there are trends towards convergence in general terms within the EMEs. Considering countries do respond to challenges in a fairly path-dependent way, this is not surprising. Yet innovations in governance set within new or emerging contexts have always brought about change. So whereas the historical sources of divergence may have declined, states are always seeking innovative solutions to the changing problems they face. And with the narrow focus on EMEs presented here, it is important to keep in mind that greater generalizability may be difficult, and further research that explores a full range of states across time will be necessary if meaningful conclusions are to be made about capitalist types.

NOTES

1. Exceptions would include Hong Kong or Singapore, which skipped the ISI stage altogether and went directly to export promotion. However, these two states do not belong to the current cohort of emerging economies in this research.
2. The core of the VoC framework is the concept of institutional complementarities. Two economic institutions can be defined as complementary if the presence of one increases the efficiency or returns from the other (Hall and Soskice 2001, 17). For example, short-term capital requires fast entry and exit from markets, but to do so requires a flexible labor market, which in turn attracts more capital.

6 The Qualitative Comparative Analysis (QCA) Research Process

Remaining parsimonious while at the same time identifying how complex systems interact can be a challenge for any type of research.[1] To manage these complexities, I analyze how economic institutions matter by using two complementary research methods: Qualitative Comparative Analysis (QCA) and quantitative regression. Incorporating innovative methods such as QCA into a range of mixed-method approaches is supportive of the trend to employ different and more demanding techniques for explicit, transparent and rigorous measurement. Although by no means pervasive, these are important developments that help to encourage a more ambitious and sophisticated methodological repertoire within and across the social sciences.

In an effort to develop the cumulative capacity to diagnose and mediate the problems associated with linked socio-economic and ecological systems, this chapter provides an introduction to the QCA approach. Many scholars understand that single cases are important; at the same time, many of them also aspire to produce generalizations. QCA is an approach that allows the investigator to pursue both of these previously contradictory goals. As with all techniques, however, QCA has its limitations. A major goal of this research is to illustrate the strengths and weaknesses of this increasingly popular methodology. To achieve this goal, Chapter 6 begins with a brief history and overview of the QCA approach. I also demonstrate the six steps used in the QCA research process. In doing so, I hope to illustrate key aspects and applications of this method. Clearly, the better use we can make of the methodological toolbox available to us, the more accurate and reliable will be the conclusions we can reach.

A. WHAT IS QUALITATIVE COMPARATIVE ANALYSIS (QCA)?

QCA is a comparative method that uses a logical process of systematically paired comparisons to derive the various pathways to a common outcome in a complex system. Research based on paired comparisons has a long-standing tradition in comparative politics. For example, this is the same underlying logic found in Mill's Method of Difference (Mill 1843/2009).

QCA is considered a synthetic methodology because it has elements of both qualitative (case-oriented) and quantitative (variable-oriented) approaches. As a result, the method can take on a reasonably large number of cases ($n \approx 100$), while remaining rigorous and parsimonious.

QCA uses the binary logic of Boolean algebra to identify common causal patterns within diverse configurations of social phenomena. Boolean algebra is a logic-based empirical approach developed by George Boole (1847) in the 1840s as a means to study binary phenomena. It resembles linear algebra, but its purpose is to allow the researcher to use mathematical logic to substitute for verbal reasoning.

Using formal logic statements, the cases under consideration are represented as a combination of causal and outcome conditions that can be mapped and assessed as a score on the dependent variable for that case. In his earlier work, Charles Ragin (1987) found that several different combinations of causal factors led to the presence of a democratic state. By using QCA, the combinations found within these instances of democratic governance could also be logically simplified through a case-by-case process of comparison. What emerged were sets of causal "recipes" that produced necessary and/or sufficient outcomes of the phenomena under study.

Although it is not a new research method, QCA has gained popularity since being revolutionized by Charles Ragin (1987, 2006) and computer programmer Kriss Drass. Although originally used by electrical engineers to simplify switching circuits (Quine 1952), the Boolean approach found in QCA today is increasingly used across a variety of fields in the social sciences. For example, QCA has been used to show the necessary and sufficient conditions for a variety of social phenomena including the causes of revolutions (Skocpol 1980; Wickham-Crowley 1991; Foran 2005), democratic transitions (Schneider and Wagemann 2006), patterns of economic development (Katz, vom Hau, and Mahoney 2005) and, most recently, globalization (Ignatow 2011).

The causal patterns identified using QCA are not the finished product. Instead, they serve to group similar cases together to show how varying sets of causal conditions combine to produce similar outcomes. Because QCA can only highlight patterns in the data, an additional phase of interpretive analysis is required. As discussed below, this additional phase is highly beneficial because it creates a valuable feedback loop in the research process that encourages further refinement and specification of the theoretical model. As a consequence, QCA permits both theory (deductive reasoning) and empirical data (inductive reasoning) to influence the overall conclusions of the research.

B. APPLYING THE QCA APPROACH

The main benefit of the QCA approach is its ability to simplify complexity by identifying patterns of attributes that produce a successful or unsuccessful outcome. There are six key steps in the application of the QCA method.

Six Steps in the QCA Research Process:

1. Identify positive and negative cases or outcomes
2. Identify relevant causal conditions (independent variables)
3. Resolve contradictions in the model
4. Find the solution formula and minimize
5. Assess the fit of the model
6. Determine necessary and/or sufficient conditions

Step 1: Identify Positive and Negative Cases.

Research begins by classifying cases along the dependent variable to identify all positive and negative outcomes. For this research, cases of successful market formation are identified by the standards established in Chapter 4. Cases that meet the criteria for success are identified as positive cases. The negative cases are also identified following the same process. Cases that do not meet the established standard are identified as negative cases. Through this process, six positive cases are established: Argentina, Brazil, China, Colombia, India and Indonesia. The remaining twenty-five cases are considered negative and include the following states: Bahrain, Bangladesh, Botswana, Chile, Cyprus, Egypt, Jordon, Kenya, Macedonia, Malaysia, Mauritius, Mexico, Morocco, Nigeria, Pakistan, Peru, Philippines, Qatar, Serbia, South Africa, Sri Lanka, Thailand, Tunisia, UAE and Vietnam.

Defining the positive and negative cases allows the researcher to begin the process of clustering cases into like categories. Cases that do not fall clearly into this binary classification system can still be managed using QCA. First, the researcher begins with binary sets called "crisp-sets" (csQCA). If greater variation is necessary, "fuzzy-sets" (fsQCA) can be used. Fuzzy-sets are groups whose units have degrees of membership in a category (i.e. they are scaled within the category and are no longer dichotomous). As illustrated in Table 6.1, fuzzy-sets can be used to extend crisp-sets by permitting scaled

Table 6.1 Crisp-Sets versus Fuzzy-Sets

Crisp set (csQCA)	Three-value fsQCA	Four-value fsQCA	Six-value fsQCA	Continuous fsQCA
1 = fully in	1 = fully in	1 = fully in	1 = fully in	1 = fully in
0 = fully out	0.5 = neither fully in nor fully out	0.67 = more in than out	0.9 = mostly, but not fully in	0.5 < more in than out < 1
	0 = fully out	0.33 = more out than in	0.6 = more or less in	0.5 = cross-over: not in or out
		0 = fully out	0.4 = more or less out	0 < more out than in < .5
			0.1 = mostly, but not fully out	0 = fully out
			0 = fully out	

membership scores between zero and one (Ragin 2000). In other words, if further degrees of specification are necessary, fuzzy-sets allow the researcher that needed flexibility.

For this research, the crisp-set form of QCA is used for several reasons. First, additional degrees of specification are not necessary within this model. Second, csQCA allows for a direct comparison with the standard binary logistical regression model, helping to elucidate the strengths and weaknesses of QCA versus other statistical approaches. Finally, csQCA is the most parsimonious avenue to understanding how complex systems of economic institutions interact.

Step 2: Identify Causal Conditions

In step two, the researcher identifies all the theoretically relevant causal conditions that are expected to influence the outcome variable. As illustrated in Table 6.2, the relevant causal conditions are the variables described previously. They include the dependent variable for successful CDM market formation (DV) and the five independent variables derived from the Varieties of Capitalism (VoC) literature: labor relations, finance, inter-firm relations, education and vocational training and corporate governance.

Once operationalized and measured, each variable must be specified regarding its presence or absence in the case. This is described with the aid of a membership function valued in the real unit interval set [0, 1]. A score of one indicates a condition is present and a score of zero means that the condition is absent. The binary output from the dichotomization process produces the data matrix found in Table 6.2.

For the outcome (DV), a score of one indicates a case of successful CDM market formation, whereas zero signifies the absence of success. For the causal conditions (e.g. independent variables), a score of one suggests the presence of a Liberal Market Economy (LME) characteristic. A zero suggests the absence of the LME characteristic and therefore suggests the presence of a Controlled Market Economy (CME) characteristic because the two ideal types are considered opposite ends of a common scale.

In Table 6.2, cases have been grouped first by the dependent or outcome variable (DV) and then by identical combinations of conditions. By grouping the data in this way, the table is easier to read and interpret. Also, Grofman and Schneider (2009) suggest that by presenting this data first in the spreadsheet format, with variables as columns and cases as rows, a common starting point for later comparison can be established.

Next, I advance to the more customary data presentation format used in QCA, which is illustrated in Table 6.3. In this case, the binary output from the dichotomization process produces what is called a "truth table." A truth table is a matrix used to display and compute the functional values of logical expressions across each of the cases. In other words, truth tables are used as a way to organize, illustrate and formalize the process of case comparison.

Table 6.2 Data Matrix of VoC Conditions—Crisp-Set

Country	Level of Dev	VoC A	VoC B	VoC C	VoC D	VoC E	DV
Argentina	3	0	0	0	1	0	1
Brazil	1	0	0	1	0	0	1
China	2	0	0	0	0	0	1
Colombia	2	0	0	1	1	1	1
India	2	0	1	1	1	1	1
Indonesia	2	0	1	0	0	0	1
Bahrain	3	1	1	0	1	1	0
Bangladesh	3	1	0	0	0	1	0
Botswana	3	1	0	0	0	0	0
Chile	2	1	1	1	1	1	0
Cyprus	3	0	0	1	1	0	0
Egypt	2	0	0	0	0	0	0
Jordan	3	1	1	0	1	0	0
Kenya	3	1	0	0	0	0	0
Macedonia	3	0	0	0	0	0	0
Malaysia	1	1	1	1	1	1	0
Mauritius	3	1	0	1	0	1	0
Mexico	1	0	0	1	1	0	0
Morocco	2	0	0	0	0	0	0
Nigeria	3	1	0	0	0	1	0
Pakistan	2	1	0	0	0	1	0
Peru	2	0	0	0	0	1	0
Philippines	2	0	0	0	1	0	0
Qatar	3	1	1	1	1	0	0
Serbia	3	1	0	0	0	0	0
So. Africa	1	0	1	1	1	1	0
Sri Lanka	3	0	0	0	0	0	0
Thailand	1	1	0	1	1	1	0
Tunisia	3	1	0	1	1	1	0
UAE	2	1	1	1	1	0	0
Vietnam	3	0	0	0	0	0	0

Note: VoC A = labor relations; VoC B = finance; VoC C = inter-firm relations; VoC E = education and training; VoC E = corporate governance; and DV = successful market formation. Level of Dev: 1 = Advanced Emerging, 2 = Secondary Emerging, 3 = Frontier Emerging

This enables the researcher to transparently identify explicit connections between combinations of conditions and outcomes so the most fundamental causes of the outcomes can be exposed.

Table 6.3 Truth Table of VoC Condition Variables

	Conditions						Outcomes		
	VoC A	VoC B	VoC C	VoC D	VoC E	# of cases	DV	Con Score	Cases
1	0	0	1	1	1	1	Success	1	Colombia
2	0	0	1	0	0	1	Success	1	Brazil
3	0	1	0	0	0	1	Success	1	Indonesia
4	0	1	1	1	1	2	Contradiction	0.5	India, South Africa
5	0	0	0	1	0	2	Contradiction	0.5	Argentina, Philippines
6	0	0	0	0	0	6	Contradiction	0.17	China, Egypt, Macedonia, Morocco, Sri Lanka, Vietnam
7	1	1	1	1	1	2	Failed	0	Chile, Malaysia
8	1	1	1	1	0	2	Failed	0	Qatar, UAE
9	1	1	0	1	1	1	Failed	0	Bahrain
10	1	1	0	1	0	1	Failed	0	Jordon
11	1	0	1	1	1	2	Failed	0	Thailand, Tunisia
12	1	0	1	0	1	1	Failed	0	Mauritius
13	1	0	0	0	1	3	Failed	0	Bangladesh, Nigeria, Pakistan
14	1	0	0	0	0	3	Failed	0	Botswana, Kenya, Serbia
15	0	0	1	1	0	2	Failed	0	Cyprus, Mexico
16	0	0	0	0	1	1	Failed	0	Peru
17	1	1	1	0	1	0	LR		
18	1	1	1	0	0	0	LR		
19	1	1	0	0	1	0	LR		
20	1	1	0	0	0	0	LR		
21	1	0	1	1	0	0	LR		
22	1	0	1	0	0	0	LR		
23	1	0	0	1	1	0	LR		
24	1	0	0	1	0	0	LR		
25	0	1	1	1	0	0	LR		
26	0	1	1	0	1	0	LR		
27	0	1	1	0	0	0	LR		
28	0	1	0	1	1	0	LR		

(*Continued*)

Table 6.3 (Continued)

	Conditions					Outcomes				
	VoC A	VoC B	VoC C	VoC D	VoC E	# of cases		DV	Con Score	Cases
29	0	1	0	1	0	0	LR			
30	0	1	0	0	1	0	LR			
31	0	0	1	0	1	0	LR			
32	0	0	0	1	1	0	LR			

Note: VoC A = labor; VoC B = finance; VoC C = inter-firm relations; VoC D = ed/training; VoC E = corporate governance; DV = outcome; Con Score = Consistency Score; LR = Logical Remainder

The truth table presented here covers the five VoC variables or conditions (as they are called in QCA). The truth table lists all the logically possible combinations of conditions and outcomes associated with the research frame. On the left side of the truth table, each row represents one of 2^k logically possible combinations of the binary k conditions. On the right side of the truth table are all the possible outcomes of interest. The right side of the table begins with the column called "# of cases" which expresses the number of cases containing the unique causal recipe in each row. Next is the column "DV," which shows the dependent or outcome variable (as it is called in QCA). This is followed by the consistency score, which tells us how consistent this causal pattern is with the outcome it is related to. This will be explained in greater detail in step three. Last is the column specifying the cases or countries related to the combinations of conditions and outcomes in each row.

The truth table illustrates several parts of the dataset. It begins with all possible logically derived combinations. In this case, that would be 2^5 (representing the 5 VoC variables and their possible binary outcomes) totaling thirty-two possible combinations. Of these combinations, three (rows 1–3) are linked as sufficient conditions for the occurrence of successful CDM market formation. Likewise, ten combinations covering eighteen cases (rows 7–16) are linked to its failure.

In addition, three combinations covering ten cases (rows 4–6) are considered mixed or contradictory cases because a contradictory outcome has occurred for a similar combination of the causal recipe. In other words, a successful case matches the same characteristics of an unsuccessful case. As a result, these sets of conditions are not considered sufficient for the presence or absence of successful CDM market formation. More importantly, because contradictory configurations correspond to ten out of thirty-one cases, this presents us with some important information. In this case, economic institutions, as I have defined them, are not the only factors at play. This is an important fact that will be fleshed out further during the final analysis.

The remaining rows of the truth table are what is referred to as the logical remainders of the "truth-functional logic-derived" universe of potential cases. In other words, rows 17–32 in Table 6.3 are simply the hypothetical or logically derived, but unobserved cases. They are combinations not found in the sample, but that may logically exist (e.g. in a larger sample). What this illustrates is a concept called limited diversity. In essence, not all logically possible outcomes have been empirically observed, and so they are considered, for this project, to be logical remainders. Interestingly, limited diversity is a common feature of all comparative approaches.[2] Normally, if limited diversity is not observed, the research is considered suspect and the model must be refined.

Step 3: Resolve Contradictions in the Model

Because a portion of the cases in my sample were found to be contradictory, the third step is to streamline the model. This is an important feature of QCA because it allows the researcher to adapt the model within the research process. In other words, at this stage, the coherence of the model may be assessed and the causal conditions and measures reevaluated. The ability to check the coherence of the variables is a powerful tool that is common to quantitative analysis. In statistical terms, this is similar to finding the "goodness of fit" for a model. The better the goodness of fit, the better our empirical model appears to explain the data. In the end, this process improves parsimony, strengthens the theoretical framework, and improves the specification of the model.

To begin this process, first the contradictory configurations must be resolved. Although contradictions are common (e.g. cases that are identical with respect to causal conditions, but different outcomes), they do not falsify the theory under investigation. In fact, these contradictions shed further light on the causal conditions that are truly relevant to the theory. As Rihoux and Ragin (2009, 16) point out, "[b]y seeking a solution to these contradictions, the researcher will get a more thorough knowledge of relevant cases and develop a more coherent body of evidence."

To address these contradictions, variables are added or removed, creating a valuable feedback loop that is resolved once the theoretical frame is strongly supported by the model. To address this, the control variables are added to the baseline model described as "VoC" in Table 6.4. The basic VoC model, if you recall from Table 6.3, exhibited three sufficient, three contradictory and ten total failed configurations.

Through this first set of consistency tests, variable CON H (public institutions) can be removed. This occurs because the number of sufficient, contradictory and failed configurations has not been improved over the basic model with the addition of this variable. Likewise, although there appears to be some improvement in the model through variable CON G (infrastructure), it must also be removed. This is required because there

Table 6.4 Testing the QCA Models

Variable	Successes	# Contradictions	# Failed
VoC	3	3 (0.5, 0.5, .17)	10
VoC and CON F	5	1 (0.33)	16
~~VoC and CON G~~	4	2 (0.5, 0.17)	12
~~VoC and CON H~~	3	3 (0.5, 0.5, 0.20)	13
VoC and CON I	5	1 (0.5)	12

Note: VoC = 5 VoC variables; CON F = macroeconomic stability; CON G = infrastructure; CON H = public institutions; CON I = population

are two other variables that appear to resolve the contradictions while covering all the other cases as well. This suggests that a more parsimonious solution exists.

What is also shown is Table 6.4 is that there are two remaining variables for consideration: CON F and CON I. The variable CON F (macroeconomic stability) is the only variable to resolve the contradiction found between Argentina and the Philippines. The former has a high score on the variable and the latter a low one. By the same token, the variable CON I (population) best resolves the two remaining contradictions for China and India. Once the contradictions are satisfactorily resolved, the theoretical frame is strongly supported by the conditions in the model. Next, a contradiction-free truth table is created. A partial version of this new truth table is found in Table 6.5.

The contradiction-free truth table lists all the logically possible combinations of conditions and outcomes associated with the research frame. In this case, that would be 2^7 (representing the seven independent variables and their possible binary outcomes), totaling 128 possible combinations. Of the 128 possible combinations, six (rows 1–6) are linked as sufficient conditions for the occurrence of successful CDM market formation. Likewise, seventeen combinations covering twenty-five cases (rows 8–24) are linked to its non-occurrence or failure.

The remaining rows of the truth table (which are not pictured in this example) are logical remainders. They are combinations not found in the sample, but that may logically exist (e.g. in a larger sample). Because we have no theoretical knowledge on which to determine the outcomes for these logical remainders, we cannot address them further here. However, there are ways to use logical remainders for counterfactual thought experiments in situations where theory can be used to infer possible outcomes for specific causal conditions. This has been the approach used in QCA models of democracy formation, for example. In these cases, historical evidence is used to infer specific patterns as a means to imply likely outcomes.

Table 6.5. Partial Truth Table of VoC Conditions, Plus CON F and CON I

	Conditions								Outcomes		
	VoC A	VoC B	VoC C	VoC D	VoC E	Con F	Con I	#cases	DV	Con Score	Cases
1	0	1	1	1	1	0	1	1	Success	1	India
2	0	1	0	0	0	0	0	1	Success	1	Indonesia
3	0	0	1	1	1	0	0	1	Success	1	Colombia
4	0	0	1	0	0	0	0	1	Success	1	Brazil
5	0	0	0	1	0	1	0	1	Success	1	Argentina
6	0	0	0	0	0	1	1	1	Success	1	China
7	1	1	1	1	1	1	0	2	Failed	0	Chile, Malaysia
8	0	0	0	0	1	0	0	1	Failed	0	Peru
9	0	0	0	1	0	0	0	1	Failed	0	Philippines
10	1	1	1	1	0	1	0	2	Failed	0	Qatar, UAE
11	1	0	0	0	0	0	0	2	Failed	0	Kenya, Serbia
12	0	0	1	1	0	0	0	1	Failed	0	Mexico
13	0	0	1	1	0	1	0	1	Failed	0	Cyprus
14	0	0	0	0	0	1	0	2	Failed	0	Macedonia, Vietnam
15	1	0	0	0	1	0	0	3	Failed	0	Bangladesh Nigeria, Pakistan
16	0	0	0	0	0	0	0	3	Failed	0	Egypt, Morocco, Sri Lanka
17	0	1	1	1	1	1	0	1	Failed	0	South Africa
18	1	0	0	0	0	1	0	1	Failed	0	Botswana
19	1	0	1	0	1	0	0	1	Failed	0	Mauritius
20	1	0	1	1	1	0	0	1	Failed	0	Tunisia
21	1	0	1	1	1	1	0	1	Failed	0	Thailand
22	1	1	0	1	0	0	0	1	Failed	0	Jordon
23	1	1	0	1	1	1	0	1	Failed	0	Bahrain

Note: VoC A = labor relations; VoC B = finance; VoC C = inter-firm relations; VoC D = education and vocational training; VoC E = corporate governance; CON F = macroeconomic stability; CON I = population; DV = successful CDM market formation; Con Score = Consistency Score

Step 4: Find the Solution Formulas and Minimize

Once the contradiction-free truth table is complete, the researcher begins to string together the logic equations representing each individual case found in the sample. According to Grofman and Schneider (2009, 664), "The most frequently used and, for all practical purposes, obligatory way of expressing the results of QCA is to write them down in the form of a solution formula, the end product of the process of logically summarizing/encapsulating the information stored in the truth table." That is to say, a solution formula written in mathematical notation is used to enable further simplification of the results. This is done using Boolean algebra to find the most encompassing and parsimonious outcome possible. The following section will demonstrate how the solution formula is derived using Boolean techniques.

Boolean algebra is a logic-based empirical approach that resembles linear algebra. However, instead of numeric operations (+, −, *, /) it uses the logical operations of conjunction (x∩y), disjunction (xUy) and negation (−x). The Boolean operations include these and all other operations that can be created from using them together in combination. This generally leads to a finite set of possible outcomes that fall on a range of zero to one.

An example that I believe helps to understand the Boolean approach is the concept of Venn diagrams. A Venn diagram is an illustration that shows all possible logical relations between finite collections of sets. This is literally all we are producing when using QCA. Basic examples of the logical operators found in QCA are illustrated in Figure 6.1 below.

In a solution formula, these three operators provide all the variability that is logically necessary to simplify large batches of binary data. In a

<table>
<tr><td>The combined area of two sets (X and Y) is called the union of set X and set Y. This is denoted by X ∪ Y. In QCA, this is expressed as logical OR (+). It is used when at least one of the sets is present.</td><td>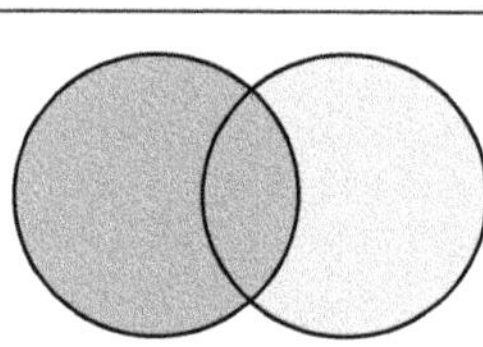</td></tr>
<tr><td>The area where the two sets overlap is called the intersection of X and Y. This is denoted by X ∩ Y. In QCA, this is expressed as logical AND (*). Intersection results from being in both set X and set Y.</td><td>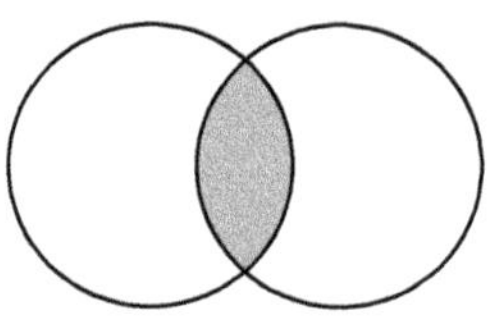</td></tr>
<tr><td>The final operator found in QCA is called negation and is denoted by a negative sign (–). In QCA, this is called logical NOT. This occurs from membership in one set but not the other.</td><td>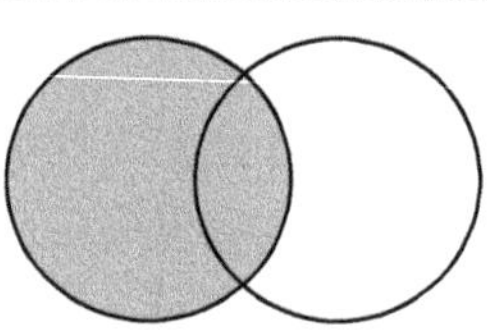</td></tr>
</table>

Figure 6.1. Venn Diagrams of the Three Basic QCA Operators

QCA solution formula, letters are used to replace the numbers they represent, and then are linked using the Boolean operators.[4] Letters associated with a logical NOT are illustrated with lower-case letters, whereas logical OR and logical AND are illustrated by upper-case letters. Using the described approach, it is possible to specify a solution formula for the sufficiency of the outcome in this research (e.g. successful CDM market formation).

To summarize the outcome, each of the causal recipes from the successful cases (rows 1–6 of the truth table found in Table 6.5) are expressed using the letters that correspond to the condition variables they represent. These are referred to as primitive expressions. Next, each primitive expression is strung together using the appropriate Boolean operator. The primitive expressions from Table 6.5, when strung together with Boolean operators, produce equation 1:

$$aBCDEfI + aBcdefi + abCDEfi + abCdefi + abcDeFi + abcdeFI \rightarrow DV \quad (1)$$

Each of these primitive expressions represents a combination of causal conditions found in at least one instance of successful CDM market formation. Each term is a product of the conditions (A*B*C*D*E*F*I) because they represent the intersection of conditions that together produce an outcome. They are no longer considered individually, but are instead considered as a set—as prescribed by the VoC theory. This is the meaning behind the concept of conjunctural causation. The ability to study causation in sets is a unique benefit of QCA, as it allows the researcher to study phenomena holistically.

The arrow found at the end of the equation serves three purposes. First, it avoids the use of the equal sign (generally used in quantitative regression analysis) as a way to signal a divergent method. This is required because QCA is often compared with quantitative approaches or used in mixed method research designs. In addition, the presence of the arrow indicates that the expression to its left implies the outcome to its right. Finally, it illustrates that these data can be seen as sufficient conditions for the outcome (Grofman and Schneider 2009, 665). In other words, the logical expression described above includes all the causal combinations that produced a successful outcome from the set.

Next, the rules of Boolean minimization are used to reduce the primitive expression as much as possible. To do this, each individual expression is compared with the other expressions in the formula. Equations that differ by the presence or absence of just one attribute are treated as equivalent, with the contradictory attribute removed from the equation. For example, if Y = ABC + ABc, it would be simplified to Y = AB because C/c are both present and absent in the outcome. The logic of this simple data reduction parallels the logic of experimental design because the varying condition (C/c) is not influencing the dependent or outcome variable.

The process of minimization continues in a stepwise fashion until no further reductions of the Boolean expressions are possible. The product terms produced using this simple minimization rule are called the "prime implicants." In algebra, this is similar to reducing the equation to its simplest form—the lowest common denominator. The prime implicants are essentially the most relevant variables within the model. They include all the patterns that result after eliminating the logically irrelevant factors.

With small datasets, this is possible to do by hand, but with larger ones, the QCA software must be employed. Consequently, I will illustrate this process with a simple example. First, I begin with a set of primitive expressions that produce the following solution formula:

$$\text{MtF} + \text{mTf} + \text{MTf} + \text{MTF} \rightarrow \text{Y} \tag{2}$$

Using the described minimization techniques, the expression MtF and MTF would produce the reduced expression "MF." Likewise, mTf and MTf would produce "Tf" and MTf and MTF produce "MT." Through this process, the equation can be reduced to the set of prime implicants shown in equation 3:

$$\text{MF} + \text{Tf} + \text{MT} \rightarrow \text{Y} \tag{3}$$

Through this same process, the primitive expression for my research (equation 1) can also be reduced. The prime implicants for my dataset are found in equation 4. For my data, however, none of these combinations vary by just one condition. Therefore, the primitive expressions cannot be reduced any further by hand through the minimization process. This is common with smaller, complex datasets. However, by using the QCA software, greater levels of parsimony can be reached. This will be demonstrated further in Chapter 7.

$$\text{aBCDEfI} + \text{aBcdefi} + \text{abCDEfi} + \text{abCdefi} + \text{abcDeFi} + \text{abcdeFI} \rightarrow \text{DV} \tag{4}$$

Once the prime implicants for each case have been derived, they are simplified further through a process called "implication." This is possible because each prime implicant covers (or implies) several primitive expressions in the truth table. The implication process works to reduce complex sets to their most parsimonious form, while still implying or covering all the causal combinations in the cases. In algebra, this is similar to factoring equations. If one expression is a subset of another, then it is implied by or included within the other. For example, A implies Abc because Abc is a subset of A.

What is commonly found in QCA research is that some prime implicants cover more than one factor. That is, they overlap, and some are unnecessary if the researcher's goal is to be parsimonious. To address this, the model must be streamlined to remove any redundancies. In order to determine which prime implicants are logically essential, a prime implicants chart may be used. The goal of the implicants chart is to "cover" as many of the primitive expressions as possible with the minimum number of prime implicants that are required to successfully cover all the positive outcomes.

To demonstrate the minimization device, let me return to the "simple" example. Recall the solution formula given previously:

$$MtF + mTf + MTf + MTF \rightarrow Y \quad (5)$$

As well as the final set of prime implicants produced through the process of minimization from this example:

$$MF + Tf + MT \rightarrow Y \quad (6)$$

From this example, a prime implicants chart is produced and shown in Table 6.6.

From this chart, a final covering equation is reported as the following:

$$MF + Tf \rightarrow Y \quad (7)$$

This final expression is considered the most parsimonious logical outcome for describing the different combinations of conditions associated with the positive outcome. That is, this is the expression that includes the least number of combinations that still cover all the conditions that produce the positive outcome. The final reduced equation shows the two (logically minimal) combinations of conditions that cause Y (the outcome variable), and thus it provides an explicit statement of conjunctural causation.

Once this detail is known, however, the research process does not stop there. Another benefit of QCA is the concept of asymmetrical causation. This is one of the many ways that QCA is well suited for the study

Table 6.6 Prime Implicants Chart Example

Prime Implicants	**Primitive Expressions**			
	MtF	mTf	MTf	MTF
MF	X			X
Tf		X	X	
MT			X	X

of real-world phenomena. QCA allows the research to study both the patterns that produce an outcome and the patterns that do not produce an outcome—without the assumption that they are exact opposites.

In quantitative or correlation-based approaches, it is assumed that causation is one directional or "symmetrical." If X causes Y, then the lack of X is not expected to produce Y. However, it is easy to imagine issues in social science where this is just not the case. For example, a good education often produces a high income, but not every PhD student gets a good job. Social science is filled with such examples.

In QCA, causation is not symmetrical, as I will demonstrate now. Accordingly, the final step requires the researcher to go logically from successful outcomes to a model of unsuccessful ones. There are two ways to do this. First, when working with QCA logic by hand, it is possible to work through the process in reverse by searching for the patterns of failure and then reducing them. As an alternative, this can be done mechanically by use of what is called De Morgan's Law. This mathematical law includes a pair of transformation rules derived from inference that enables conjunction and disjunction via negation (Copi, Cohen, and McMahon 2011). De Morgan's Law is a shortcut for getting to negative instances by logic rather than actual empirical study of cases.

To understand this better, I refer again to the "simple" example provided above where the following minimized equation was produced:

$$MF + Tf \rightarrow Y \qquad (8)$$

If this equation was recoded using De Morgan's law, everything would be essentially changed to its opposite (M becomes m, F becomes f, T becomes t, f becomes F and Y becomes y). Next, the logical operators are also switched. Recall that logical OR implies addition and logical AND implies multiplication. For example, MF (M*F) becomes M+F. Together, this produces the following minimized formula for the failed outcomes in this example:

$$(m + f)(t + F) \rightarrow y \quad \text{where } y = \text{the unsuccessful outcome of } Y \qquad (9)$$

This reduces to the following formula:

$mt + mF + ft \rightarrow y$ Note: fF is dropped; because in logic, it is not possible for a factor to be present and absent. (10)

This final expression is considered the most parsimonious logical outcome for describing the different combinations of conditions associated with the negative outcome. What are represented are three possible explanations for why the outcome is not successful. Importantly, none of these explanations are found to be exact opposites of the configurations that produced the positive outcome. This finding illustrates the concept of asymmetrical causation in QCA.

Employing the QCA Software

Due to the complexity of the data required for this research project, computing by hand would be a daunting task and the risk of error would likely be high. Luckily, the same analysis can also be done using the Boolean algorithms in the fsQCA 2.0 software (Ragin, Drass and Davey 2006). In addition, over the past five years, QCA analytical software has also been made available for STATA and the R statistical package. Due to the complexity of the model explored in this research, the fsQCA software 2.0 will be used to reduce the solution formula to its prime implicants and analyze its output.

When using the fsQCA software, some additional analysis is also enabled. In particular, three solution options—complex, parsimonious and intermediate—are available, and will be demonstrated here. In addition, some very important measures of fit are also provided, which will be analyzed in step five. I begin with the most complex solution offered for the data output, which is demonstrated in Table 6.7.

The complex solution is essentially the full model without any implication or applied counterfactuals. What Table 6.7 illustrates, first of all, is the model found in this research project. Next, the method used to analyze these data, referred to as the Quine-McCluskey algorithm, is identified. The assumptions delineated here are these: a) only cases that actually exist in the dataset can be counted (case frequency ≥ 1); and b) only fully consistent

Table 6.7 Complex Solution—Extended VoC Model

****

TRUTH TABLE ANALYSIS

****

Model: dv = f(voca, vocb, vocc, vocd, voce, conf, coni)
Rows: 23
Algorithm: Quine-McCluskey
True: 1
--- COMPLEX SOLUTION ---
Frequency cutoff: 1.000000
Consistency cutoff: 1.000000

	Raw Coverage	Unique Coverage	Consistency
aBcdefi	0.166667	0.166667	1.000000
abCdefi	0.166667	0.166667	1.000000
abcDeFi	0.166667	0.166667	1.000000
abcdeFI	0.166667	0.166667	1.000000
abCDEfi	0.166667	0.166667	1.000000
aBCDEfI	0.166667	0.166667	1.000000

Solution coverage: 1.000000
Solution consistency: 1.000000

variable combinations are considered successful (consistency cutoff = 1). Here, consistency indicates that each prime implicant used in this analysis has only one outcome—either positive or negative. In other words, each combination is consistently producing one binary outcome (e.g. success or failure). Both assumptions can be adjusted depending on the amount of cases and the various needs of the QCA researcher.

In addition, three measures of coverage and an overall consistency score are provided. These measures will help to analyze the overall fit of the model in step five. Hence, both concepts will be described in greater detail there. What can also be noted from the complex solution is that the final combinations resemble the primitive expressions and solution formula reached previously by hand. However, because one goal of this research is to reduce the complexity of the data, this is not the most appropriate solution for this research project.

The second solution provided using the QCA software is the parsimonious solution. This solution indicates which conditions are essential to distinguish between the cases. This is done by using both positive and negative cases, plus counterfactuals based on the logical remainders found in the truth table. To do this, the software employs a logic-based algorithm that attempts to reduce the table until no further simplification is possible. It will then display all of the possible choices in the solution.

As may be recalled from the prime implicant chart shown in Table 6.6, what often occurs is that there are more resulting prime implicants than are needed to cover all the original primitive expressions. If the algorithm is run and the table cannot be fully reduced, the QCA software allows the researcher to choose from among those that are "logically tied" or overlapping using the prime implicant chart. In order to remove any redundancies and determine which prime implicants are logically essential, the user may select the prime implicants that make the most sense based on theoretical and substantive knowledge. The one exception is that all essential prime implicants (e.g. those that cannot be covered through other means) are required in the final solution and therefore, must be included. For these data, Table 6.8 shows the prime implicants chart produced for the parsimonious solution set.

What emerges from the prime implicants chart produced by this parsimonious solution is the following: first, only five total prime implicants are required to fully cover the model. The countries of Indonesia, Colombia, Brazil and Argentina can be covered by several different options (between two and four prime implicants each). This is possible because the prime implicants produced from the truth table are considered logically equivalent if they cover the same rows in the truth table. If a solid body of evidence regarding the mechanics of the economic institutions in these states already existed, the researcher could make decisions as to which made most sense. Conversely, both India and China can only be covered by one essential prime implicant. Here, the variable for high population (I) on its own is considered the only means to cover both these cases. Such findings do

Table 6.8. Prime Implicants Chart for the Parsimonious Solution

	Prime Implicants		Primitive Expressions			
	India	Indonesia	Colombia	Brazil	Argentina	China
	aBCDEfI	aBcdefi	abCDEfi	abCdefi	abcDeFi	sabcdeFI
I	X					X
Bd		X				
aBf		X				
aBe		X				
aBc		X				
Cde				X		
aCd				X		
aCEf			X			
abCE			X			
aDEf			X			
abDE			X			
cDeF					X	
bcDF					X	
acDF					X	

not bode well for the thesis that economic institutions alone determined the outcomes in these two cases.

Because there is so little substantive knowledge as to how to theoretically apply covering variables by implication on this subject, it is very difficult to proceed with this solution. Here, the parsimonious solution will require a complex interpretation where substantive knowledge just does not exist yet. Nonetheless, this information does provide a starting point for future research and theory building. Hence, like Goldilocks, I move on to the solution that is just right for this project.

"One strength of QCA is that it not only provides tools for deriving the two endpoints of the complexity/parsimony continuum, it also provides tools for specifying intermediate solutions" (Ragin 2008, 51). The solution presented here is one example of an intermediate solution. To derive this solution, the software conducts counterfactual analyses based on causal conditions supplied by the user. There are two types of counterfactuals possible—easy and hard. Easy counterfactuals are based on existing knowledge that supports or infers an outcome. Hard counterfactuals are not. They may be based on logic or probability, but rarely on observed evidence.

I have chosen to use only easy counterfactuals in my data analysis because it produces the same solution as what a conventional case-oriented researcher would derive from the evidence based on stepwise comparative analysis. This same logic is what produces the optimal intermediate solution in the fsQCA software. According to Ragin (2008), to achieve this, each counterfactual assumption must be 1) shared by the positive cases (or at least a subset of the positive cases); 2) believed to be linked to the outcome and 3) not displayed by negative cases.

Hence, the counterfactuals used in this intermediate solution analysis include the positive and negative cases and the presence of the variable for high population (CON I). The solution produced through these assumptions appears in Table 6.9. The logical remainders are not used in this instance because so little is actually known about how economic institutions function within emerging economies. Nonetheless, this does give some guidance for future research and suggests that larger samples for further comparison may be useful. Once some patterns are established, incorporation of logical remainders to produce counterfactual arguments may also have greater potential.

As the intermediate solution indicates, there are six sufficient causal combinations. Together, they produce the final solution formula:

abCdef + aBcdef + abceFI + abcDeF + abCDEf + aCDEfI → DV (11)

Although this looks fairly similar to the complex solution previously presented in equation 4, equation 8 has been further minimized with the help of the counterfactuals. As established in Table 6.9, rows 1, 2, 4 and 5 no

Table 6.9 Intermediate Solution—Extended VoC Model

```
**********************
*TRUTH TABLE ANALYSIS*
**********************
Model: dv = f (voca, vocb, vocc, vocd, voce, conf, coni)
Rows: 31
Algorithm: Quine-McCluskey
True: 1, 0 Matrix: 0L, Don't Care: -
--- INTERMEDIATE SOLUTION ---
Frequency cutoff: 1.000000
Consistency cutoff: 1.000000
Assumptions: Con I (present)
```

	Raw Coverage	Unique Coverage	Consistency
abCdef	0.166667	0.166667	1.000000
aBcdef	0.166667	0.166667	1.000000
abceFI	0.166667	0.166667	1.000000
abcDeF	0.166667	0.166667	1.000000
abCDEf	0.166667	0.166667	1.000000
aCDEfI	0.166667	0.166667	1.000000

Solution coverage: 1.000000
Solution consistency: 1.000000

longer contain the variable CON I (high population). Also, row 3 no longer contains the variable VoC D (education and vocational training). And row 6 no longer contains the variable VoC B (finance). Hence, not all of the VoC variables still play a positive or negative part in two of the cases. These findings will be discussed further in Step 5. To make the connections between the final solution formula and the actual countries explicit, a prime implicants chart is presented in Table 6.10.

Analysis of the Negation of the Outcome

Although the main goal of this research is to understand the role of economic institutions in successful CDM market formation, failed formation is just as informative and should not be expected to produce opposite or symmetrical findings. As Schneider and Wagemann (2010, 409) suggest, "[s]uch analyses can help to grasp the causal logic driving the positive cases and/or generate substantively interesting insights in their own right."

As previously illustrated, the solution formula for the non-occurrence of an outcome can be derived by applying De Morgan's law. However, De Morgan's law will not produce a logical solution formula if the truth table contains any logical remainders or contradictory rows (Schneider and Wagemann 2007, 112.). Although all contradictions were removed from the truth table prior to the analysis, logical remainders did result. Consequently, this dataset requires a separate analysis in which the negative outcome is specified as the phenomenon to be explained. Using the same assumptions and model, only negated, the intermediate solution can also be studied, as illustrated in Table 6.11.

The intermediate solution produces the following solution formula:

$$\text{Bcdei} + \text{bcdfi} + \text{abDefi} + \text{AbCEfi} + \text{AbCDEi} + \text{BCDEFi} + \text{ABDEFi} + \text{ABCDFi} + \text{ABcDefi} \rightarrow \text{dv} \quad (12)$$

Table 6.10 Prime Implicants Chart for the Intermediate Solution

Prime Implicants	Primitive Expressions					
	India	Indonesia	Colombia	Brazil	Argentina	China
	aBCDEfI	aBcdefi	abCDEfi	abCdefi	abcDeFi	abcdeFI
abCdef				X		
aBcdef		X				
abceFI						X
abcDeF					X	
abCDEf			X			
aCDEfI	X					

Table 6.11 Intermediate Solution for the Failed Cases

Model:~dv = f(coni, conf, voce, vocd, vocc, vocb, voca)
Rows: 24
Algorithm: Quine-McCluskey
True: 1, 0 Matrix: 0L, Don't Care:

--- INTERMEDIATE SOLUTION ---

frequency cutoff: 1.000000
consistency cutoff: 1.000000
Assumptions: ~coni (absent)

	Raw Coverage	Unique Coverage	Consistency
Bcdei	0.320000	0.120000	1.000000
Bcdfi	0.360000	0.160000	1.000000
abDefi	0.080000	0.080000	1.000000
AbCEfi	0.080000	0.040000	1.000000
AbCDEi	0.080000	0.040000	1.000000
BCDEFi	0.120000	0.040000	1.000000
ABDEFi	0.120000	0.040000	1.000000
ABCDFi	0.160000	0.080000	1.000000
ABcDefi	0.040000	0.040000	1.000000

Solution coverage: 0.960000
Solution consistency: 1.000000

As in the positive cases, the prime implicants found among the negative cases cannot be reduced further because each of the prime implicants uniquely covers at least one case each. Finally, a quick comparison of the solution formula for positive cases (equation 8) and the solution formula for negative or failed cases (equation 9) illustrates this phenomena is indeed asymmetric. In other words, what causes successful CDM market formation has very little in common with what prevents it.

Step 5: Assess the Fit of the Model

The fifth step in the research process is to assess the measures of fit for the model. There are two main parameters used in QCA, and they include the concepts of consistency and coverage. The measure for consistency gauges the degree to which the cases sharing a given combination of conditions agree in producing the outcome in question (Ragin 2008), whereas coverage gauges the degree to which a cause or causal combination "accounts for" instances of an outcome. "When there are several paths to the same outcome, the coverage of a given causal combination may be small. Thus coverage suggests empirical relevance or importance" (Ragin 2008, 44). Figure 6.2 illustrates these two concepts.

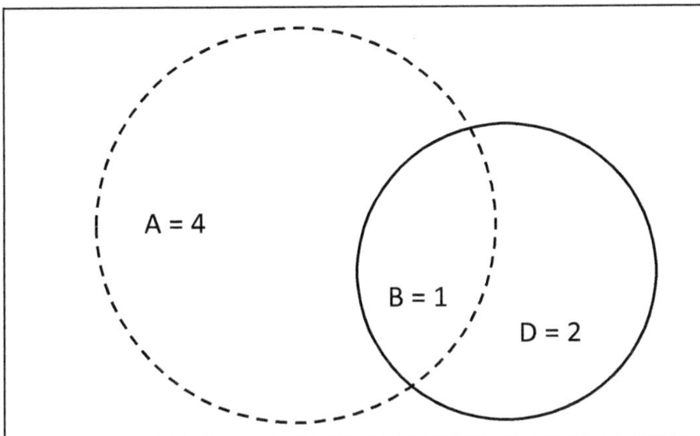

A = the outcome of interest. Consistency is the proportion of B relative to D (B/(B + D)). Coverage is how much B overlaps with A (B/(A + B)).

Figure 6.2 Venn Diagram of Consistency and Coverage Concepts in QCA

Consistency and coverage in QCA are easily related to two other concepts in quantitative research. This includes the measures of significance and strength of correlation. In short, consistency behaves like significance—telling the researcher if an empirical relationship is of interest. If the consistency score is low (generally below 0.75) then the empirical relationship may be spurious.[5]

Coverage, like the strength of correlation concept, indicates the empirical relevance of the connection. However, it is vital to understand an important distinction regarding coverage. Although coverage measures only empirical importance, this does not diminish its possible theoretical relevance. As one author notes, "[a] sufficient relation may be quite 'rare' from an empirical point of view (and thus exhibit low coverage), but it still could be centrally relevant to the theory. For example, the sufficient relation might be proof that a path that was thought to be empirically impossible, at least from the perspective of theory, in fact is not." (Ragin 2008, 55).

If we now refer back to the measures of fit produced through the intermediate solution in Table 6.9 (for the positive cases) and Table 6.11 (for the negated cases), we are able to describe these concepts. The summary of these statistics for the positive cases are illustrated in Table 6.12.

Because only fully consistent cases were included in the model, each prime implicant produces a consistency score of one. The other measure of consistency is the solution consistency, which tells us the degree to which membership in the solution (the set of solution terms) is a subset of membership in the outcome. Because all the solution terms are fully consistent, the solution consistency is also equal to one for the successful cases.

Table 6.12 Summary of Consistency and Coverage Score—Positive Cases

Prime Implicants	aCDEfI	aBcdef	abCDEf	abCdef	abcDeF	abceFI	→ DV
Consistency	100%	100%	100%	100%	100%	100%	
Raw coverage	17%	17%	17%	17%	17%	17%	
Cases covered	India	Indonesia	Colombia	Brazil	Argentina	China	
Unique coverage	17%	17%	17%	17%	17%	17%	
Cases uniquely covered	India	Indonesia	Colombia	Brazil	Argentina	China	
Solution consistency							100%
Solution coverage							100%

Reaching full consistency is not as common as it might appear. This is much harder to do with larger, less complex or more similar datasets. Plus, I have been able to streamline the model by testing the alternative variables proposed previously. Having a strong consistency (e.g. like the idea of significance) suggests that this relationship is of interest and not just random. However, high consistency scores do not necessarily mean that an important relationship exists.

Once it has been determined that a set of conditions is sufficient (or consistent) in the processes of explaining the outcome, the coverage parameter is tested. Coverage can be defined as the proportion of cases with successful outcomes displaying a specific condition or combination of conditions relative to the number of overall cases. The higher the coverage score, the more that is being explained by the condition or set of conditions. This is the same idea as what was previously illustrated by the Prime Implicants Chart in Tables 6.6 and Table 6.8 above.

To assess coverage, three different measures are used. The first measure of coverage is the solution coverage, which is similar to the overall solution consistency. This measure tells us the proportion of membership in the outcome that is explained by the complete solution. As Table 6.12 shows, the intermediate solution for the successful cases found six out of six successful cases produced consistent outcomes. Hence, the solution coverage, or overall coverage, was 6/6 = 100%.

The second measure of coverage is called the raw coverage score. In this case, each condition, or set of conditions, is given a raw coverage score that measures the total number of original or primitive expressions covered by the combination. For the positive cases, each combination was equal to

1/6 = 0.166667. Although there is no set standard for high and low coverage, this is clearly on the lower end.

The final measure of coverage is called the unique coverage. This measure details all the cases covered by that unique condition or combination of conditions alone. For the positive cases, the unique coverage scores for each combination was also equal to 1/6 = 0.166667. Like the measure for raw coverage, these lower unique coverage scores do not suggest a strong correlation in the model. But because the scores are all equal, none stands out as overly dominate in the model either.

In short, the model for the positive or successful cases displays a strong consistency, but low coverage, across the solution terms. This is very similar to a finding in more conventional empirical research of a significant, but weak correlation. In QCA, this outcome occurs when the proposed causal combinations are complex, producing several unique pathways—none of which dominate overall. However, it is very important to remember that coverage gauges only empirical importance, which does not diminish its possible theoretical importance. As previously mentioned, sufficient relations are sometimes rare from an empirical point of view (and thus exhibit low coverage). For example, considering that only six out of thirty-one cases in my sample were considered successful at CDM market formation, this would hold well with the results produced. Hence, such findings should still be considered relevant.

If we now refer back to the measures of fit produced through the intermediate solution for the negated or failed cases found in Table 6.11, the goodness of fit for that model can also be described. The summary of these statistics are shown in Table 6.13. What first emerges when exploring the coverage for the negative or unsuccessful cases is how the result varies dramatically from the positive cases. This is a great illustration of the asymmetry of social phenomena.

Beginning with the solution coverage for the negative cases found in Table 6.13, it appears that twenty-four out of twenty-five unsuccessful cases produced consistent outcomes. Only the case of Cyprus was not sufficiently covered by the solution formula. Hence, the solution coverage or overall coverage was 24/25 = 96%.

For the negative cases, the raw coverage has much more variety; however, the overall percentage also remains somewhat low. In fact for four of the prime implicants, the coverage score is below 0.08, which is a very low score. Two additional prime implicants for the negative cases fall between 0.12–0.16, these include the following: BCDEFi, ABDEFi and ABCDFi. However, two of the prime implicants, bcdei (0.32) and bcdfi (0.36), have coverage scores above 30%.

The unique coverage scores also reflect greater variation than found in the positive cases. In general, the unique coverage scores are approximately half the level of the raw coverage scores. This suggests the unique coverage is lower for the negative cases, but the raw coverage is higher.

In the unsuccessful cases, there appears to be a strong consistency with moderate coverage scores across at least two prime implicants. These are

Table 6.13 Summary of Consistency and Coverage Solution—Failed Cases

Prime Implicants	bcdei	bcdfi	abDefi	AbCEfi	AbCDEi	BCDEFi	ABDEFi	ABCDFi	ABcDefi	→ DV
Consistency	100%	100%	100%	100%	100%	100%	100%	100%	100%	
Rawcoverage	32%	36%	8%	8%	8%	12%	12%	16%	4%	
Casescovered	Botswana Egypt Kenya Macedonia Morocco Serbia Sri Lanka Vietnam	Bangladesh Egypt Kenya Morocco Nigeria Pakistan Peru Serbia Sri Lanka	Mexico Philippines	Mauritius Tunisia	Thailand Tunisia	Chile Malaysia S. Africa	Bahrain Chile Malaysia	Chile Malaysia Qatar UAE	Jordon	
Unique coverage	12%	16%	8%	4%	4%	4%	4%	8%	4%	
Cases uniquely covered	Botswana Macedonia Vietnam	Bangladesh Nigeria Pakistan Peru	Mexico Philippines	Mauritius	Thailand	S. Africa	Bahrain	Qatar UAE	Jordon	
Solution consistency										100%
Solution coverage										96%

significant enough to stand out. The contrast of the positive and negative causal combinations and coverage are quite striking, yet they also share some similarities too. However, the interpretation of these outcomes will be discussed in step six.

Step 6: Identifying Necessary and/or Sufficient Conditions

In the last step of the research process, the final solution formula derived from the prime implicants is used to determine the relationship between the causal conditions and the outcome of interest. In QCA, this is done by understanding what variable or sets of variables are necessary and/or sufficient to produce the outcome. A condition is necessary if it is always present when the outcome occurs. A cause is sufficient if it can produce a certain outcome.

As Benoit Rihoux and Charles Ragin (2009, 10) so eloquently put it, "a given path toward an outcome usually consists in a combination of conditions that is sufficient (a sufficient combination or 'intersection' of conditions) to produce that outcome. However, that path is not always necessary, as some other alternative paths (with different conditions, at least partly) could very well produce the same outcome." Table 6.14 helps to illustrate the logic of necessary and sufficient conditions.

To access necessary and sufficient conditions, I return to the minimized intermediate solution formula for my positive cases included here:

$$abCdef + aBcdef + abceFI + abcDeF + abCDEf + aCDEfI \rightarrow DV \qquad (13)$$

From this solution formula, it is understood that there are six sufficient paths leading to successful CDM market formation, each corresponding to one country each. The presence of the logical OR (+) in the equation indicates that each of these figures is considered sufficient to produce the outcome. The logical AND (*) separating the sets of conditions indicates that what causally matters are not the individual conditions, but these specific combinations of them.

Table 6.14 Identifying Necessary and/or Sufficient Conditions (Ragin 1997)

Y = AC + Bc	No cause is either necessary or sufficient
Y = AC + BC	C is necessary but not sufficient
Y = AC	Both A and C are necessary but not sufficient
Y = A + Bc	A is sufficient but not necessary
Y = B	B is both necessary and sufficient

Although the minimal descriptive formulas produced through the QCA approach are still quite complex, they do provide some preliminary interpretations. For example, macroeconomic stability (F) and population (I) were found to play an important role in successful CDM market formation among the EMEs. More importantly, the VoC variable for education and vocational training (D/d) does not play a role in the outcome for China, whereas the VoC variable for finance (b/B) does not play a role in the case of India. Because both finance and education are VoC variables, this suggests that other priorities may also be at play in the institutional setting faced by EMEs. In fact, for China and India, the variable for high population played a greater role than two types of economic institutions in determining outcomes.

Despite these preliminary findings, it is important to keep in mind that QCA is a configurational method that requires the full causal recipe to determine causation. In other words, focusing on the role of individual conditions in isolation from the other conditions violates the fundamentals of causation in QCA, and should be done with caution. Luckily, by studying these phenomena using a mixed-method research design, these findings can also be compared and verified with, in this case, a more common quantitative approach.

In addition, no conclusions in QCA can be made without also examining negative cases. To better understand the unsuccessful cases, I return to the minimized intermediate solution formula for the negative cases:

$$\text{Bcdei} + \text{bcdfi} + \text{abDefi} + \text{AbCEfi} + \text{AbCDEi} + \text{BCDEFi} + \text{ABDEFi} + \text{ABCDFi} + \text{ABcDefi} \rightarrow \text{dv} \quad (14)$$

From the intermediate solution formula for the negative cases, it is understood that there are nine sufficient paths covering twenty-five countries that lead to unsuccessful CDM market formation. Again, the presence of the logical OR (+) in the equation indicates the combinations of sufficient conditions, and the logical AND (*) separating the sets of conditions, indicates that what causally matters are not the individual conditions, but these specific combinations of them.

Again, the minimal descriptive formulas produced for the negative cases can provide some useful insights. Interestingly, the commonly shared condition among the failed cases is low population (i). This helps to illustrate how the necessary condition is not always causally relevant. For example, it may be found that air is necessary for a stable democracy to form, but that does not make it causally relevant. In this case, there are good reasons why a high population might spur a country to take action in environmental markets. Indeed, countries with higher populations are one of the groups that will bear larger burdens from climate change and adaptation. However, there are also small island populations that will be gravely influenced as well. Hence, population size seems less causally relevant for the negated cases.

If the findings for the positive and negative cases are compared, other interesting findings are produced. For example, all six positive cases were found to contain highly regulated labor relations. However, only two of the twenty-five failing cases also contain this pattern. This is a powerful finding as it suggests that coordinated labor plays an important role in determining environmental outcomes, among other things. However, because QCA does not have the benefit of statistical certainty, further studies and evidence will be required prior to making any major conclusions. Luckily, by using a mixed-method research design, I am able to overcome that weakness using a quantitative approach to verify these findings.

One clear benefit of the QCA approach that emerges from this overview is that the methodology allows systematic cross-case comparison beyond small-n cases studies, while still preserving within-case complexity. Understanding the six sufficient patterns of success and nine sufficient patterns of failure has helped to gain some degree of parsimony in these cases. More importantly, the cases have shed new light on how these characteristics interact. For example, the solution formula for positive and negative cases illustrates that what causes successful CDM market formation has very little in common with what prevents markets from forming. Such findings promote improved empirical classification and aid in concept building and theory development. Likewise, the issue of error measurement and poor generalization illustrate some of the weaknesses of this method, which will be explored next in Chapter 7.

NOTES

1. For details on the quantitative and qualitative debate see Brady and Collier (2004). For a complete discussion on the limits of qualitative and quantitative methods, see King, Keohane, and Verba (1994) and Ragin (1997).
2. For information on limited diversity see Schneider and Wagemann (2006) or Ragin (1987).
3. For information on limited diversity see Schneider and Wagemann (2006) or Ragin (1987).
4. Boolean operators: logical OR (union +), logical AND (intersection *) and logical NOT (negation –).
5. Statistically speaking, $n \geq 10$ before a researcher can truly be confident that the findings hold (e.g. 4/4 = 100% consistence, but this does not have the same weight as the example 19/22 = 86% consistency, but in the second case, the scores are lower).

7 Determinates of Market Formation

Applying a Mixed-Method Approach

The overall premise of this book is that the variation of success we find in environmental outcomes among the emerging markets is due to the type of economic institutions prevalent in their economies. In the preliminary analysis presented in Chapter 5, it was found that the Varieties of Capitalism (VoC) types (e.g. Liberal Market Economies and Controlled Market Economies) not only can be found among the developing economies, but that those types may influence the success rate of certain policies there. However, such patterns do not confer why such underlying causal patterns occur. What other priorities or institutions are at play? What causes these new sources of diversity in Emerging Market Economies (EMEs)? The goal of this chapter is to explore these competing priorities and their underlying impacts.

To achieve this goal, I focus on a random sample of thirty-one EMEs using the VoC variables along with a set of controls to help explain which preexisting economic institutions, and in what combinations, produce the successful or unsuccessful creation of markets for the Clean Development Mechanism (CDM). To do so, I introduce a mixed-method research design to test how economic institutions matter in two separate ways. First, I use Qualitative Comparative Analysis (QCA) to identify the common causal patterns responsible for the success or failure of market formation. I then compare and contrast these results using a binary logistic regression to establish the statistical significance and overall fit of the model. By using this comparative mixed-method approach, I hope to strengthen my findings and highlight the benefits of the mixed method research design for explaining why some of these late industrializers have been more successful than others in addressing environmental issues.

A. THE COMPLEMENTARITY OF MIXED-METHOD APPROACHES

There is an ongoing debate in the literature over which research methods are most superior. There are some academics who argue for the rigor of quantitative approach, whereas others champion the holistic nature of qualitative research. An increasingly sophisticated option gaining traction in political science is the mixed method research design. For example, the two approaches presented in this research have strengths and weaknesses that can be mediated and improved through a mixed-method research design. If used as a set of tools and applied where most appropriate, combined methods can add potentially valuable knowledge regarding complex social phenomena. Especially when the number of observations meets the basic requirements for statistical tests, the relative strengths and weakness of the approaches can be bolstered through the use of a mixed-method design.

One reason mixed methods work in this case is because QCA is a synthetic methodology. Subsequently, the method takes on characteristics of both the qualitative and quantitative approaches. For example, as in case studies, QCA begins with a bottom-up approach[1] that pieces cases together to illustrate a grander pattern. Then, as in quantitative research, QCA uses stepwise paired comparisons to strategically simplify complexity and expose various patterns within a system. Because QCA takes on attributes of both qualitative and quantitative methodologies, this presents some unique opportunities. For example, there are times when QCA is useful for verifying or confirming quantitative findings. Where the methods diverge, however, they can be used to compensate for each other's inherent weaknesses.

QCA and various quantitative methods also share the ability to move beyond small-n research designs. As is common in most statistical analysis, QCA can handle a reasonably large number of cases, giving it an advantage over most qualitative methods. In his award-winning book *Taking Power*, John Foran (2005) uses the QCA approach to analyze the causes behind some three dozen revolutions in the Third World between 1910 and the present. With advancements in QCA programing, however, more recent projects have efficiently tackled fifty to one hundred cases in a set. These larger sample sizes can only be matched by formal regression analysis.

Conversely, QCA and standard statistical methods have different goals when considering their research populations and overall sample size. Whereas regression seeks to maximize sample size, QCA has a preference for unit homogeneity, which requires a more defined sample. As Katz et al (2005, 540) point out, "[i]n regression studies, researchers often work with inclusive definitions of populations—for example, a population of all nation-states—that maximize degrees of freedom but risks introducing unrecognized heterogeneity into the analysis." This conflicts with the assumption of unit homogeneity expected of quantitative research. When heterogeneity is masked by this assumption in an effort to build up sample size, the causal effects of the independent variables may be incorrectly estimated and lead to an overestimation of the error term (Long 1997). Because the QCA approach must limit populations based on homogeneity, these two approaches can provide a useful system of checks and balances in the sample selection process.

There are also other ways these two methods might be considered complementary. The most important relates to how each approach addresses the issue of complexity. Whereas quantitative approaches use laser-like precision to isolate and understand individual variables, QCA's strengths fall at the opposite end of the scale. Instead, the QCA approach gives a premium to detecting sets of conditions or pathways to a common outcome. These differences can be attributed to how each method assumes causation. Whereas standard statistical methods assume linear causation, QCA assumes necessary and sufficient causation, including combinations of jointly sufficient causes—what is referred to as conjunctural causation. In other words, in QCA, there is an expectation that "logical conjunctions of conditions or in additive combinations (not single variables in isolation) are causally relevant for producing the outcome" (Grofman and Schneider 2009, 666). Thus, a more specific understanding of the necessary and sufficient causal conditions is required.

The QCA model also assumes equifinality. In other words, QCA begins with the assumption that there may be many pathways or sets of causal terms required to get to a given outcome. In contrast, quantitative approaches expect that the same weighting of a combination of factors will explain the given outcomes. By beginning with a more holistic approach, QCA can explore each case systematically "because it views cases in terms of combinations of values and compares their different combinations holistically—making it ideal for identifying patterns of multiple conjunctural causation" (Ragin 1997, 101). I find this to be more reflective of real life phenomena.

Because these two approaches address complexity differently, QCA can be used as an organizing framework early on in the research process. As a useful first step in a research design, for example, QCA can be helpful for managing causal complexity. One important way it does this is through the solution formulas produced by Boolean notation, which aid in conceptualizing complex phenomena. This is especially helpful in the theory-building portions of the research process. Here, QCA provides alternative perspectives of the data so that appropriate categories can be considered and alternative hypotheses can be explored. It also helps in confirming the sequence of processes and pinpointing intervening and causal mechanisms, as I will demonstrate later in this chapter.

Another benefit of QCA's approach to complexity is that it can also be used to help narrow the research field, highlighting important causal factors or thresholds for more rigorous testing during later stages of the research process. In contrast, quantitative analysis is excellent for testing and fine-tuning the model in the final stages of research once a more parsimonious model has been developed. Together, these two approaches can work to preserve the complexity of the underlying phenomena of interest while simplifying the analysis as much as possible.

A final way these two methods complement each other is their diverging approaches to data. In regression, a strict science-based protocol is used in the collection of data. Variables are measured on nominal, ordinal or interval scales or must be converted to them. Data are expected to be reliable and objective, therefore missing data can create a statistical nightmare and extreme values are seen as atypical outliers. Research, accordingly, tends to become data-driven and diverted away from issues that lack the requisite base of quantifiable information. In effect, scientific method plays a key role in defining what will be studied, automatically marginalizing grander questions that cannot be reduced to a manageable set of regressions.

In contrast, QCA approaches data and measurement quite differently. In QCA, all types of data can be incorporated, thus missing data can be filled in from other sources of empirical evidence. Furthermore, QCA views cases with extreme values as crucial and highly representative instances of a phenomenon. "This mode of measurement encourages researchers to infuse causal factors and outcomes with theoretical and substantive knowledge, by assigning measurement values in ways that reflect specific research goals" (Katz et al 2005, 540). This is possible because in crisp-set QCA, the data must be scaled from zero to one to facilitate the use of set-theory and notation, thus simplifying the data early on in the research process.

This simplification process, also known as dichotomization, is seen as a weakness of the approach by some researchers because the process may cause a loss of information as the data is simplified. However, this ignores the larger picture. Every form of empirical scientific inquiry—whether qualitative or quantitative—requires some form of simplification.[2] In addition, many variables can easily be dichotomized in a simple manner when dealing with the presence or absence of some phenomenon (De Meur and Rihoux 2002). For example, the presence or absence of an actor is often easy to determine. The need for greater complexity in such cases is not warranted. In such situations, De Meur and Rihoux (2002) argue that simplification through dichotomization actually allows the researcher to make progress in the comprehension of complexity, without the loss of overall knowledge.

Also, the issue of dichotomization is another area where quantitative methods can be combined to strengthen the QCA approach. In cases where it is not clear how to dichotomize data, then a whole range of reliable techniques can be drawn from quantitative approaches. And with the recent improvements in the QCA software, graduated outcomes can easily be produced and compared with their statistical counterparts. This allows the researcher to determine if dichotomization or gradual scales are most appropriate, while allowing for improved parsimony when possible.

There are many similarities in the ways quantitative and QCA approaches evaluate the strength of the empirical support for the arguments they are specifying. By using both in a mixed-method research design, the systematic case-by-case comparison approach can be extended beyond small-n studies, while still preserving within case complexity. QCA can also extend the narrow research agenda driven by the hard science approach to data in quantitative techniques. In turn, statistical approaches can create reliable and objective avenues for dichotomization and provide important tests of significance. Together, these approaches can achieve improved generalization to help overcome issues concerning measurement error as well. Such insights are especially useful in the study of social scientific phenomena.

B. APPLYING THE MIXED-METHOD RESEARCH DESIGN

In the field of International Political Economy, where there are currently around 200 economies, innovative tools that can explore complex phenomena of real importance with medium sized samples are increasingly required. I find the QCA approach, when combined with standard statistical procedures, to be a great advancement for understanding complex interconnected systems. By employing this framework, I hope to illustrate the similarities and differences between these two methodological approaches—neither of which I see as intrinsically superior. In fact, much of what determines their success has to do with the number of cases and causal factors, the type of data available or the type of hypotheses tested.

When using a mixed-method research design, it is important to recognize some important distinctions between the various approaches. One important distinction is that regression and QCA models make different assumptions about the nature of causation and, therefore, test for different types of hypotheses. For example, regression models usually formulate hypotheses under the assumption that a given independent variable might probabilistically increase or decrease values of a dependent variable, controlling for the effect of all other variables. This happens because in regression research, analysts often assume linear causation and attempt to estimate the average effect. The understanding of causation here is one of linear covariation and, ultimately, correlation.

In contrast, the QCA approach requires hypotheses where a given causal factor, or even combinations of jointly connected causes, might be necessary or sufficient for an outcome. For example, a classic necessary causation hypothesis would argue that a minimal level of economic development is a prerequisite for democracy. For sufficient causation, where multiple pathways to an outcome might be possible, a hypothesis might propose that a minimum level of economic development *or* a strong rule of law are the only two pathways to democracy. These differences in causation influence the formulation of distinct research questions and hypotheses between these two methods.

Perhaps the most important distinction between the two approaches, however, is the assumption of asymmetric causality. In QCA, the researcher must assume that the occurrence of a phenomenon and its nonoccurrence require separate analyses. In other words, what causes markets to succeed and fail are not just opposites. They have unique causes that may be quite literally unrelated in terms of the causal factors that produce them.

The asymmetry of social phenomena is a factor that Charles Ragin (1987, 1997, 2000, 2006) has emphasized throughout his work. In his earliest books on QCA, Ragin (1987, 2000) argued that most social scientists believe that set-theoretic arguments must be reformulated as symmetric correlational arguments to be valid and testable (e.g. adding a cause-and-effect variable to prove the correlation). However, this is what requires us to take the phenomenon of interest out of its context to be studied. Instead, Ragin argues that real-life phenomena are embedded within their context and, therefore, not reliably patterned. Social scientists need to look for consistent connections that are nonlinear, that is, "causally relevant commonalities that are more or less uniformly present in a given set of cases" (Ragin 1987, 2).

Asymmetric hypothesis testing, however, requires a trade-off that might not make sense in some research. Whereas QCA is good at evaluating conditions within set-based relations, this means the technique is inadequate for detecting correlations, which is the strength of most quantitative approaches. As I will demonstrate, the result is that these two methods are not able to test the same types of hypotheses. These differences, however, are actually a great advantage to the researcher; together, they can help to verify and strengthen the findings produced, no matter which type of hypotheses are used. To illustrate this, the following section provides a demonstration of how the QCA and conventional quantitative approaches can easily be combined to produce a superior understanding of the phenomena being studied.

QCA Analysis

To apply the QCA method, the six-step research process is undertaken as described in Chapter 6. First, the positive and negative outcomes are identified. Cases that meet the criterion for success are identified as positive cases and cases that do not meet the established standard are identified as negative cases. Through this process, six positive cases are established: Argentina, Brazil, China, Colombia, India and Indonesia. The remaining twenty-five cases are considered negative and include the following states: Bahrain, Bangladesh, Botswana, Chile, Cyprus, Egypt, Jordon, Kenya, Macedonia, Malaysia, Mauritius, Mexico, Morocco, Nigeria, Pakistan, Peru, Philippines, Qatar, Serbia, South Africa, Sri Lanka, Thailand, Tunisia, UAE and Vietnam. Defining the positive and negative cases allows the researcher to begin the process of clustering cases into like categories.

Next, the researcher identifies all the theoretically relevant causal conditions that are expected to influence the outcome variable. As described in Chapter 4, this includes the dependent variable for successful CDM market formation (DV), the five independent variables derived from the Varieties of

Capitalism (VoC) literature and the four control variables derived from the development literature.

In step three, the goal is to streamline the model by removing all logical contradictions found in the current model. To address these contradictions, control variables are added or removed to the baseline "VoC" model. The control variables include macroeconomic stability, infrastructure, strength of public institutions and population size. As described in detail in Chapter 6, while streamlining the model, the variables CON F (macroeconomic stability) and CON I (population) were found to resolve the contradictions of the baseline QCA model. Once the contradictions are satisfactorily resolved, the theoretical frame is strongly supported by the conditions in the model.

Next, a contradiction-free truth table is created. This enables the researcher to transparently identify explicit connections between combinations of conditions and outcomes so the most fundamental causes of the outcomes can be exposed. It is at this stage that the researcher begins to string together the logic equations representing each individual case found in the sample. Due to the complexity of the data at this stage, the QCA software 2.0 (Ragin, Drass and Davey 2006) is used to reduce the solution formula to its prime implicants and analyze its output.

As described in detail in Chapter 6, the intermediate solution formula is used because it has the best balance between plausible and factual considerations. The assumptions used for analyzing the logical remainders include the following: each counterfactual assumption must be 1) shared by the positive cases (or at least a subset of the positive cases); 2) linked to the outcome and 3) not displayed by negative cases. The solution produced through these assumptions shows that there are six sufficient causal combinations that lead to a positive outcome. Together, they produce the final solution formula in equation 1.

$$\text{abCdef} + \text{aBcdef} + \text{abceFI} + \text{abcDeF} + \text{abCDEf} + \text{aCDEfI} \rightarrow \text{DV} \tag{1}$$

Although the main goal of this research is to understand the role of economic institutions in successful CDM market formation, failed formation is just as informative and should not be expected to produce opposite or symmetrical findings. As Schneider and Wagemann (2010, 409) suggest, "[s]uch analyses can help to grasp the causal logic driving the positive cases and/or generate substantively interesting insights in their own right." Using the same assumptions and model, only negated, the intermediate solution for the failed cases is found to produce the following solution formula for the negative cases:

$$\begin{aligned}&\text{Bcdei} + \text{bcdfi} + \text{abDefi} + \text{AbCEfi} + \text{AbCDEi} + \text{BCDEFi}\\ &\quad + \text{ABDEFi} + \text{ABCDFi} + \text{ABcDefi} \rightarrow \text{dv}\end{aligned} \tag{2}$$

A quick comparison of the solution formula for the positive cases (equation 1) and the negative or failed cases (equation 2) illustrates this phenomennon is indeed asymmetric. Not one sufficiency condition is found to be the opposite in the positive cases. In other words, what causes successful CDM market formation has very little in common with what prevents it.

In the last step of the research process, the final solution formula derived from the prime implicants is used to determine the relationship between the causal conditions and the outcome of interest. In QCA, this is done by understanding what variable or sets of variables are necessary and/or sufficient to produce the outcome.

To access necessary and sufficient conditions, I return to the minimized intermediate solution formula for my positive cases shown in equation 1. From this solution formula, it is understood that there are six sufficient paths leading to successful CDM market formation, each corresponding to one country each. From the intermediate solution formula for the negative cases in equation 2, nine sufficient paths covering twenty-five countries are found to produce unsuccessful CDM market formation. To verify these findings, a binary logistic regression is also considered.

Quantitative Analysis

As a comparison to the QCA analysis, the following section introduces the quantitative approach that will be used to study the data for this research. Conveniently, both methods are able to share the same dataset and theoretical frame. This is helpful in the research process because the findings will be based on literally the same data.

To begin the analysis, I start with a review of the variables for this research. The dependent variable (DV) is a nominal dichotomous variable describing if a case is successful or unsuccessful at CDM market formation. Cases are classified as 1 = successful or 0 = unsuccessful. This is determined by the three-part matrix described previously in Chapter 4. The established protocol produces six (19.4%) successful cases and twenty-five (80.6%) unsuccessful cases of CDM market formation. The descriptive statistics for the dependent variable are included in Table 7.1.

Table 7.1 Descriptive Statistics for the Binary Model

	DV	VoC A	VoC B	VoC C	VoC D	VoC E	CON F	CON G	CON H	CON I
N Valid	31	31	31	31	31	31	31	31	31	31
Mean	.19	.48	.29	.42	.48	.42	.42	.35	.45	.06
Std. Dev	.402	.508	.461	.502	.508	.502	.502	.486	.506	.250

Like the QCA model, the basic binomial logit model for the independent variables includes the five VoC variables. To repeat, these are labor relations (A), finance (B), inter-firm relations (C), education and vocational training (D) and corporate governance (E). In addition to the main VoC variables, this analysis uses the same control variables that were presented in the QCA model. These additional controls include macroeconomic stability (F), infrastructure (G), public institutions (H) and population (I).

The VoC variables and the control variables are dichotomous, ordinal scale variables used to illustrate the main economic institutions that determine outcomes in capitalist economies. The proposed measures have been operationalized and then scaled to an index with a range of one to seven. To dichotomize the dataset, cluster analysis was used across all the variables. In all cases, a high score on the variable is associated with a Liberal Market Economy (LME) characteristic. Likewise, a low score is associated with a Controlled Market Economy (CME) characteristic. High and low rankings of these two types were chosen at random and do not hold any special significance. Hence, cases are classified across all five VoC variables as 1 = LME and 0 = CME. The descriptive statistics for these data are also included in Table 7.1.

To understand if economic institutions determine market outcomes, a binary logistic regression is the most appropriate regression model for this research for a number of reasons. First, this model is chosen because when modeling the probability of an event as a linear equation, the assumptions of the model are violated. Consequently, the parameter estimates computed from the sample will no longer be the best linear unbiased estimators (BLUE). In addition, the binary logistic regression model is able to constrain the probabilities of an event to fall between zero and one. It also allows predictors to have a diminishing effect whenever the dependent variable is at the extremes of its range (e.g. the probability is near zero or one), and uses parameter estimators that have optimum properties (e.g. lack of bias, minimum variances) (Lottes 1996).

To analyze the data, first a binary logistic regression for the basic VoC model is run. This includes the five independent VoC variables and the dependent variable of successful or unsuccessful market formation. Next, a binary logistic regression is run for each extended model, which includes the control variables (e.g. macroeconomic stability, infrastructure, strength of public institutions and population levels). Finally, a binary logistic regression of the full model with all possible variables is run. The output from this analysis is included in Table 7.3. These regression results will be explained in greater detail in the following section.

C. DETERMINATES OF MARKET FORMATION

According to the VoC theory, the main determinants of market formation should be labor, finance, inter-firm relations, education and vocational training and corporate governance. Consequently, these variables alone should produce the full range of necessary and/or sufficient conditions for the outcomes found in this research. However, inclusion of non-economic factors from outside the model may shed light on what causes new sources of diversity in EMEs. To understand how each method identifies the underlying causal patterns or determinates of market formation, I present a goodness of fit statistic for both the quantitative and QCA approaches to establish a starting point for comparison.

Comparing the Basic and Extended VoC Model

I begin by comparing the goodness of fit for the quantitative model with similar results produced through the QCA analysis. The test statistics for the binary logistic regression presented here are the Cox & Snell and Nagelkerke R^2. The Cox & Snell and Nagelkerke R^2 are estimates of the pseudo-R^2 value, which are used to tell us something similar to what R^2 tells us in ordinary least-squares (OLS) regression. In OLS, R^2 indicates what proportion of variance is accounted for in the dependent variable based on the predictive power of the independent variables in the model. However, pseudo-R^2 statistics should never be interpreted exactly this way. Technically speaking, these statistics only measure improvement over the intercept-only model, but are used here to help illustrate some basic differences between the models.

Normally, the likelihood-ratio test is used to compare the model fit across different versions of a logit model, but for simplicity across these dissimilar methods, these two measures are used instead. In particular, these measures can roughly be compared with the two measures of fit used in QCA, which were described in full detail in Chapter 6. These include the concepts of consistency and coverage. The measure for consistency gauges the degree to which the cases sharing a given combination of conditions agree in producing the outcome in question (Ragin 2008). Coverage gauges the degree to which a cause or causal combination "accounts for" instances of an outcome. Although not entirely comparable, consistency and coverage in QCA are easily related to the measures of significance and strength of correlation. Consistency behaves like significance—telling the researcher if an empirical relationship is of interest. Coverage, like the strength of correlation concept, indicates the empirical relevance of the connection.

The maximum value for the Cox & Snell is 0.75. The Nagelkerke R^2 is an adjustment of the Cox & Snell, and serves to scale the prior statistic to a maximum value of 1.0 for easier interpretation. Conveniently, the measure of coverage in QCA also scales to a maximum value of 1.0. In both cases, high values are better than low values, with higher values suggesting that the model fits increasingly well. As presented in Table 7.2, the Cox & Snell $R^2 = 0.296$ and the Nagelkerke $R^2 = 0.474$ for the basic VoC model, suggesting a model fit around forty-seven percent for the basic VoC model (e.g. the model including the five VoC variables). Also presented in Table 7.2 is the

Table 7.2 Basic VoC Model Summary

Model	Cox & Snell R Square	Nagelkerke R Square	QCA Solution Coverage Score
VoC Model	0.296	0.474	0.50

Table 7.3 Model Summary for Extended Models

Model	Cox & Snell R^2	Nagelkerke R^2	QCA Solution Coverage Score
Basic VoC Model	**0.296**	**0.474**	**0.50**
VoC & Con F	0.297	0.475	0.83
VoC & Con G	0.427	0.682	0.67
VoC & Con H	0.383	0.612	0.50
VoC & Con I	0.376	0.602	0.83
VoC & All Controls	0.539	0.861	1.00

QCA solution coverage score for this same model. Interestingly, the QCA solution score is also relatively on par at fifty percent.

If we move on to consider the extended model, the addition of the control variables should produce pseudo-R^2 scores that are lower than the basic VoC model. This would suggest a weaker fit of the model as additional, non-VoC institutions are considered. As Table 7.3 demonstrates, the proposed variations in the model produce model fitness scores that are greater than or equal to the basic VoC model. This same result is also observed by the QCA coverage scores, suggesting an improved fit with the addition of specific controls. Because a large proportion (~50%) is still explained by the theory, this does not diminish the usefulness of the standard VoC framework completely.

Interestingly, some very important nuances between the two methods are produced through this comparison. As illustrated in Table 7.4, according to the quantitative approach, the VoC model with all four control variables (line #2) produces the best fitting model for the data. The Cox and Snell and Nagelkerke scores show an improvement in the extended model in Table 7.4 because the closer the accurately predicted values are to one, the higher the associated pseudo R^2 values are going to be. However, QCA actually finds a more parsimonious solution (line #1). According to the QCA analysis, the VoC model, with the addition of Con F (macroeconomic stability) and Con I (high population), produces the best outcome—especially when sufficiency is taken into account. To fully understand this point requires a brief dissection of how each method determines the fit of the model.

Table 7.4 Model Summary for QCA Extended Models

Model	Cox & Snell R^2	Nagelkerke R^2	QCA Solution Coverage Score
1.) VoC + Con F+ CON I	0.388	0.620	1.00
2.) VoC & All Controls	0.539	0.861	1.00

To demonstrate how QCA addresses this issue, I begin by referring to the results of the QCA analysis. Based on this information, a cross-tab of the frequencies of the final six sufficient conditions was produced. This is now illustrated in Table 7.5.

What this table helps to clarify is that the QCA model is more precise in how it addresses the idea of fit in terms of sufficiency. In short, what is presented in Table 7.5 is the proposition presented by Grofman and Schneider (2009) that for sufficiency to occur, one off-diagonal cell (top right) must be equal to zero. Necessity requires the other off-diagonal cell (bottom left) to be equal to zero. For example, in matrix 1 of Table 7.5, the set of conditions produces a sufficient, but not necessary, outcome for the tested hypothesis because there is a zero in the top right box, but no zero in the bottom left box. Because the results of the QCA analysis produced six sets of sufficient conditions for each of these outcomes illustrated in Table 7.5, there is a zero in the top right corner of each of the two-by-two matrices.

A very similar chart can also be produced using the binary logistic regression results and is useful for comparing how that model assesses fit as well. To do so, the predicted probabilities produced by the binary logistic regression are also used to create a similar crosstab for comparison purposes. With the crosstab produced in Table 7.6, it is possible to understand that the goodness of fit for the regression model works differently. What we find is that the logistic regression seeks to maximize fit, regardless of how it is maximized. As Table 7.6 demonstrates, the model works to obtain the best possible outcome, which in this case means maximizing the cases that are placed on the main diagonal. This results in a predictive error with respect to sufficiency. In other words, unlike Table 7.5, the top right cell for each model shown in Table 7.6 does not contain a zero.

This is an important downside to using logistic regression. In this model, the gain to fit is at a loss to the specification of necessary or sufficient conditions. So whereas points of sufficiency and necessity cannot be violated in QCA, logistic regression seeks to maximize fit over all other preferences. In many forms of research, such predictive errors are not a major concern. But when considering the policy implications of social phenomena, this should create some reservations.

Table 7.5 Sufficiency Conditions with DV as the Outcome Variable

1) Cross-Tab Showing aCDEfI as a Sufficient Condition for the DV	not aCDEfI	aCDEfI	Total % Correct
not successful	25	0	100%
Successful	5	1	83%
N = 31	30	1	97%

2) Cross-Tab Showing aBcdef as a Sufficient Condition for DV	not aBcdef	aBcdef	Total % Correct
not successful	25	0	100%
Successful	5	1	83%
N = 31	30	1	97%

3) Cross-Tab Showing abCDEf as a Sufficient Condition for DV	not abCDEf	abCDEf	Total % Correct
not successful	25	0	100%
Successful	5	1	83%
N = 31	30	1	97%

4) Cross-Tab Showing abCdef as a Sufficient Condition for DV	not abCdef	abCdef	Total % Correct
not successful	25	0	100%
Successful	5	1	83%
N = 31	30	1	97%

5) Cross-Tab Showing abcDeF as a Sufficient Condition for DV	not abcDeF	abcDeF	Total % Correct
not successful	25	0	100%
Successful	5	1	83%
N = 31	30	1	97%

6) Cross-Tab Showing abceFI as a Sufficient Condition for DV	not abceFI	abceFI	Total % Correct
not successful	25	0	100%
Successful	5	1	83%
N = 31	30	1	97%

However, if the preferred solution proposed by QCA is run using the logistic regression model, we can see the overall improvement provided by the QCA approach. As illustrated in Table 7.7, ultimately the solution proposed by QCA not only provides an overall equivalent fit from the full

Table 7.6 Binary Logistic Regression Prediction in Crosstab

1) Model with VoC Variables	Predicted as not successful	Predicted as successful	Total % correct
not successful	24	1	96%
successful	4	2	33.3%
N = 31	28	3	83.9%
2) Model with VoC Variables, plus CON F	**Predicted as not successful**	**Predicted as successful**	**Total % correct**
not successful	24	1	96%
successful	4	2	33.3%
N = 31	28	3	83.9%
3) Model with VoC Variables, plus CON G	**Predicted as not successful**	**Predicted as successful**	**Total % correct**
not successful	24	1	96%
successful	2	4	66.7%
N = 31	26	5	90.3%
4) Model with VoC Variables, plus CON H	**Predicted as not successful**	**Predicted as successful**	**Total % correct**
not successful	23	2	92%
successful	2	4	66.7%
N = 31	25	6	87.1%
5) Model with VoC Variables, plus CON I	**Predicted as not successful**	**Predicted as successful**	**Total % correct**
not successful	24	1	96%
successful	4	2	33.3%
N = 31	28	3	83.9%
6) Model with VoC Variables, plus All Control Variables	**Predicted as not successful**	**Predicted as successful**	**Total % correct**
not successful	24	1	96%
successful	2	4	66.7%
N = 31	26	5	90.3%

Note: Cut value = 0.50; VoC variables = labor, finance, inter-firm relations, education/training and corporate governance. CON F = macroeconomic stability, CON G = infrastructure, CON H = public institutions, Alt I = population model (Model 6 of Table 7.6), but it is more parsimonious and also avoids predictive errors with respect to sufficiency and necessity.

Although it is possible to test conditional effects in regression models, the model threshold needs to be known in advance and specified with a more complex model using interaction terms. With QCA, these conditional effects will usually be more obvious just from examining the truth table. Hence, without the aid of the QCA model to provide this direction, the preferred model found using the binary logistic regression would be incorrect—as illustrated in Table 7.7.

Table 7.7 Binary Logistic Regression Prediction in Crosstab for Proposed QCA Solution (cut value = 0.5)

7) Model with 5 VoC Variables, plus CON F and CON I		Predicted as not successful	Predicted as successful	Total % correct
	not successful	25	0	100%
	successful	3	3	50%
	N = 31	26	5	90.3%

Note: VoC variables = labor, finance, inter-firm relations, education/training and corporate governance. Alt F1 = macroeconomic stability, Alt I = population

Verifying Results of the Mixed-Method Model

Even though QCA provides the sort of model specification that can improve policy-relevant research for key issues such as human health and well-being, it has weak generalizability and is unable to test for statistical significance. This makes it difficult to use QCA by itself to determine if the outcomes produced might otherwise have been produced by chance alone. By using a mixed-method approach, QCA can be used to find the most parsimonious model, delineate thresholds for interactive effects and to specify necessary and sufficient conditions. In turn, the quantitative approach can be used to verify the statistical significance of the findings produced to greatly increase confidence in such results.

To illustrate this, consider the chi-square as a formal significance test for both the basic VoC model as well as the final model produced for the QCA analysis (e.g. the five basic VoC variables, plus the variable for macroeconomic stability [Con F] and population [Con I]). The chi-square is the appropriate test statistic here because we are exploring the frequencies of mutually exclusive categories.

In this case, the null hypothesis would be that there is no difference in the frequency of occurrences between successful and failed cases. Therefore the results could simply be due to chance (H_0: $F_s = F_f$). The alternative would be that there is a difference between the successful and failed cases that cannot

Table 7.8 Chi-Square Results

Model	Chi-square	Df	Sig.
Basic VoC Model	10.897	5	0.053
VoC, plus Alt F1/Alt I	15.220	7	0.033

be caused just by chance alone (H_1: $F_s \neq F_f$). For the chi-square, the level of significance is set at p = 0.05. The obtained values for each model are shown in Table 7.8. Although this research passes the minimum threshold (n = 30) to preform statistical testing, the estimation of the error term is still not always reliable at this level. Hence, with only thirty-one observations, it is important to be conservative when interpreting the logit results.

Because the obtained value for the basic VoC model is not significant (nor does it reach the required critical value of 11.07 for five degrees of freedom), we cannot reject our null hypothesis. We must accept that the result we found could simply have been due to chance. However, for the most parsimonious model found using QCA, the obtained value is found to be statistically significant. Because the observed data do not fit with what is expected, we can say that it differs significantly enough to suggest it is not due to chance. Therefore we can reject the null hypothesis because there is less than a five percent chance that the distribution of these cases is due to coincidence.

As this chapter has helped to illustrate, the findings produced by both methods suggest that economic institutions alone do not tell the entire story about what determines CDM market formation in every case. QCA allows us to find the most parsimonious solution overall, but lacks the ability to test for statistical significance. The quantitative approach provides tests of significance, but unlike QCA, interactive and conditional effects are not obvious in regression-type models. In this case, the quantitative method can only maximize the fit of the model, introducing predictive errors that can be misleading. By using a mixed-method approach in this research, it is possible to verify with some confidence that both population and macroeconomic stability are important factors in determining CDM market creation in some cases.

By demonstrating how QCA and quantitative approaches can be combined to analyze important outcomes, I have shown how these two methods can be complementary. QCA can extend the narrow research agenda driven by the hard science approach, whereas statistical approaches can create reliable and objective avenues for dichotomization and provide important tests of significance. Although it ultimately depends on the research goals, for this project the mixed-method approach has been fruitful. Despite this, as Johan Hellström (2011, 72) points out that "the relative merits of the two methodological traditions (case-study oriented versus variable-oriented) for testing asymmetric hypotheses and exploring causal complexity is still dividing the comparative social studies research community."[3] Realizing the complementary nature of these approaches could have positive implications for the study of complex social science phenomena.

As André-Paul Frognier (2002, 146) has pointed out, "there is no ideal method in the social sciences: the trick is to achieve the best correspondence between the data that are analyzed and the technique that will be used." Instead of choosing one method over the other, I have demonstrated how the two approaches presented in this research have strengths and weaknesses that can be mediated through a mixed-method research design. If used as a set of tools and applied where most appropriate, both can add potentially valuable knowledge regarding complex social phenomena. Especially when the number of observations meets the basic minimums to perform statistical tests, these methods are well suited for mixed-method research.

NOTES

1. In a bottom-up approach, the individual base elements of the system are first specified in great detail. These elements are then linked together to form larger subsystems, which then, in turn, are linked, sometimes in many levels, until a complete top-level system is formed.
2. For a discussion of simplification, see King, Keohane and Verba (1994).
3. See, for example, Clark et al. 2006; Goertz, 2006; Seawright, 2005.

8 Findings and Implications

Since the early works of classical economists such as Adam Smith (1776), David Ricardo (1966) and John Stuart Mill (1848), political economists have thought long and hard about how to govern the national and international economic architecture. As a consequence of this long-standing tradition, it is well understood that markets have great potential as a form of economic governance. However, as this study has demonstrated, the success of market formation in the developing world depends largely on the variety of capitalism there.

To gain greater insights into how markets and institutions interact, this book has focused on a sample of thirty-one Emerging Market Economies (EMEs) to show that national variations in economic relations are central to explaining why carbon market formation has yielded more emissions-reducing projects in some countries than in others. My analysis drew on explanatory variables from the Varieties of Capitalism (VoC) literature, to which I added four control variables: macroeconomic stability, infrastructure, strength of public institutions and population. Together, these variables were used to characterize the preexisting economic institutions in each emerging economy and to explain what combinations of economic institutions produce successful or unsuccessful market formation under the Clean Development Mechanism (CDM).

A. PROJECT FINDINGS

At the onset of this book, I defined a set of four research goals. The first of these four goals begins by asking a simple, but important, question: "what are the economies of the emerging markets really like?" The aim was to highlight and expand our understanding of the types of capitalism in the EMEs. In an era where power in the global system has become increasingly diffused, the importance of nontraditional states should not be underemphasized. Not only are these countries the future drivers of markets and policies, but they are also essential to the solutions for a broad range of issues at the international level. Based on this, it is reasonable to suggest that the nature of economic institutions in emerging economies is relevant for future policy making.

To begin to understand what the types and characteristics of the VoCs in the emerging markets are really like, a typology of capitalism was developed. In addition, the issue of convergence and divergence of capitalism was examined. From this framework, several basic underlying patterns were noted. What is clear is that the Controlled Market Economy (CME) is by far the most common type of capitalism in the EMEs. Although both hybrid and Liberal Market Economy (LME) types did exist, together they account for around half of the cases in my sample.

Likewise, because CMEs were so common, pure ideal types also reigned over hybrid types. More importantly, hybrid types were found to diminish with increasing levels of development. This suggests that at least one form of convergence may be occurring. If nothing else, the substantial number of hybrid cases in the Frontier Emerging economies does seem to confirm the notion that mixed modes of coordination produce less efficient institutional complementarities. This is further supported by the fact that eighty percent of the successful cases in my sample were pure VoC types. Insights such as these are critical because they lay the groundwork for future research on the economic performance of EMEs in various domains.

The second goal of this research was to better understand market-based policy performance. What types of capitalism enabled market formation in the case of the CDM? To address this goal, I explored the creation, or formation, of CDM markets within a set of thirty-one EMEs. The most important finding in this case was that the type of capitalism does seem to matter in terms of successful policy outcomes. In particular, it was found that among the EMEs, those states with the purest types of capitalism produced the best outcomes overall. However, CMEs outperformed both LMEs and hybrid cases.

Such findings suggest that types of capitalism, regardless of the level of development, produce real and measurable results. In the case of the CDM, positive performance (e.g. formation of environmental markets) is linked to national variations in modes of capitalist production, which suggests that current international policy designs to address climate change may be shortsighted. If firms, and therefore the states wherein they reside, require differing forms of motivation to bring about change, current policy efforts may need to adapt. By improving our understanding of how to best design and implement environmental markets, we can improve their functionality over the long term.

More broadly speaking, because EMEs are fundamental for assuring the long-term sustainability of a broad range of policy issues, this research comes at a critical juncture in the evolution of international policy regimes. As the economic institutions of the EMEs are better understood, such considerations should play a greater role in the design and implementation of market-based policies. This is especially true if meaningful policy consequences are to be produced. By focusing attention on how policy tools based on market principles can be implemented, this study can serve to further inform research on policy options for solving large-scale international problems like climate change.

The third goal of this research was to explain what additional factors or sources of diversity may be involved in market formation in the emerging economies. I began by exploring if the key economic institutions that distinguish LME and CMEs determine market outcomes or if a broader range of factors are at play. To address this, I compared two models for explaining CDM uptake in the sample countries, one relying only on the economic institutions identified in the VoC literature, and the other adding four additional variables derived from the development literature. These were macroeconomic stability, infrastructure, strength of public institutions, and the effects of population.

Because EMEs may have unique priorities that differ from their industrialized counterparts, I tried to shed new light on what competing factors and sources of diversity were at play for these states. From the QCA solution formula, six sufficient paths were found to lead to successful CDM market formation, each corresponding to one country each. When both positive and negative cases were compared, all six positive cases were found to contain highly regulated labor relations (including the one LME case). However, only two of the twenty-five failing cases also contain this pattern. Because QCA does not have the benefit of statistical certainty, a binary logistic regression was also conducted to verify the final model and to improve the overall generalizability of the findings.

According to the VoC theory, the main determinates of market formation should be labor, finance, inter-firm relations, education and vocational training and corporate governance. Although the VoC variables remained essential to the model, my analysis established that non-VoC factors from outside the theory were found to matter in around half of the successful cases. For example, in Argentina, macroeconomic stability was found to be a factor in success there. For both India and China, high population was also found to play an important role in CDM market formation. More importantly, in India, the VoC variable for corporate finance no longer played a role, and in China, the VoC variable for education and vocational training also was dropped from the model. Hence, the VoC variables alone did not account for the full range of necessary and/or sufficient conditions for the observed outcomes. Findings such as these help to explain the sources of capitalist diversity and competing priorities found among the EMEs.

To understand how each method identifies the underlying causal patterns or determinates of market formation, I presented a goodness of fit statistic for both the quantitative and QCA approaches for comparison. Because QCA is able to conduct a systematic cross-case comparison on larger-than-average samples, while still preserving within case complexity, it provided some degree of parsimony. This is valuable because the six sufficient patterns of success and nine sufficient patterns of failure provide some insight on how institutions interact. For example, the solution formula for positive and negative cases illustrates that the causes of successful CDM market formation have very little in common with what prevents markets from forming. Such findings promote improved empirical classification and aid in concept building and theory development.

The final goal of this research was to demonstrate the strengths and weakness of mixed-method research designs for furthering our understanding of international and global politics. By employing both binary logistic regression and QCA as rival tools for explaining an outcome, I hoped to highlight the complementary nature of these two methods. For this book, I evaluated these two methodologies using a comparative, medium-N research design that assumes asymmetric causation and tests hypotheses based on measures of sufficiency.

The findings produced by both methods suggest that economic institutions alone do not determine market outcomes in every case. More importantly, the pathways to success and failure have very little in common. Interestingly, QCA finds the most parsimonious solution overall, but lacks the ability to test for statistical significance. Likewise, the quantitative approach provides tests of significance, but can only maximize the fit of the model, which causes predictive errors that can be misleading. Realizing the complementary nature of these approaches could have positive implications for the study of complex social science phenomena.

Through a demonstration of how QCA and quantitative approaches can be combined to analyze important outcomes, I have shown how these two methods can be complementary. By combining the two methods, we can verify, in a statistically satisfactory way, that in addition to the VoC variables, both population and macroeconomic stability are also important factors in determining CDM market formation in some cases. Most importantly, I am able to demonstrate how the QCA and quantitative approaches can easily be combined to produce a superior understanding of the phenomena being studied. Although it ultimately depends on the research goals, for this project the mixed-method approach has been fruitful. Innovative tools such as QCA, which can provide new insights into complex phenomena of real importance, offer some advantages when applied in a mixed-method research design.

Together, these four goals and their relevant findings may provide new insights into how to properly incentivize EMEs to participate in global markets. This in turn may help to improve the overall performance of important policy regimes. By improving our understanding of how to best design and implement environmental markets and their supporting institutions, we can assure their sustainability, improve their functionality and raise confidence in such measures over the long run.

B. SPECULATIONS

Whereas it was expected that the forms of capitalism that were more adaptive to markets would excel at creating and advancing them, the opposite outcome resulted in this research. To explain these findings, I begin with a brief discussion of the institutional complementarity of both the LME and CME ideal types. I speculate that it is the varying behavior of the underlying institutional complementarities of the two different ideal types found in the VoC theory that helps to explain the outcomes found in this research.

Within the VoC literature, it is argued that understanding the diversity of institutional structures, and hence the diversity of capitalist societies, requires the study of how different institutions are complementary to each other. As a reminder, two economic institutions can be defined as complementary if the presence of one increases the efficiency or returns from the other. Different sets or structures of institutions may perform equally well in spite of being comprised of very different parts and of how differently they operate. It is therefore logical to take into account the structure formed by these institutional arrangements and argue that this institutional structure defines the behavior of each type of capitalism it produces.

To illustrate how, it is helpful to review how the complementary institutions found in the two main ideal types function. On one end of the scale are the LMEs. The LME ideal type is focused on a short-term time horizon due to the central feature of finance in this model. Here, financing is generally sourced from stock markets, which require the quick movement of capital in order to incentivize stockholders and their desire for financial returns. Because corporate governance in LMEs is dictated by stockholders who drive the market, they require unregulated and flexible labor markets that allow labor to quickly move in and out of projects currently being financed. This necessitates a workforce that is broadly educated and can move between industries. Because the LMEs are organized in this manner, they are highly innovative, efficient and flexible. Together, these complementary institutions work to assure the highest returns to capital holders, thus incentivizing further funding, maximizing employment levels, and thereby compensating for the lack of long-term employment benefits that come from more regulated forms of labor markets. In sum, LMEs are organized by markets, and shareholders' concerns drive firm decision making.

On the opposite end of the scale are the CME types. In these states, firms tend to have a much longer time horizon, and this appears to play an important role in the success of CDM market formation. In contrast to LMEs, CMEs have a greater reliance on banks and debt finance as well as more stable institutional shareholdings that give them greater immunity to short-term stock market fluctuations and demands. Because financing is less likely to be sourced through markets, this reduces the drive for short-term profits. Due to the longer term time horizon for firms in CMEs, there is an incentive to provide on-the-job training and apprenticeships for employees who, like artisans, are likely to remain in their jobs for years to come. And because so much is invested into employees, there is an incentive to take care of them through health and unemployment benefits. As a result, complementary labor markets in CMEs are highly regulated, but inflexible.

Similarly, because banks, institutional investors, employees and other stakeholders are involved in the decision-making process in CMEs, corporate governance is also a coordinated affair. Consequently, firms in CMEs must be willing and able to develop strategies that appeal to this broad range of stakeholders. And because CME projects are less profit driven in the short term, this enables them to internalize externalities, such as environmental harm, into the production process. The ability to account for these additional costs over a longer time horizon enables firms to adapt gradually and further lowers the additional costs.

Understanding how the various modes of production function is instructive for illustrating how varying capitalist modes of production have systematic effects on environmental outcomes. In the case of CDM participation in emerging economies, the economic institutions related to CMEs led to greater CDM uptake. I argue that the underlying mechanism explaining this outcome relates to the time horizon associated with economic decision making in LMEs and CMEs and how the sets of institutions within the ideal types work in a complementary fashion to facilitate the production process.

Based on this logic, the LMEs, with their market focus, should not be expected to perform well in new environmental markets and this was, in fact, the case. The reason is that LMEs are more likely to externalize social concerns for the environment because they are held hostage by their need to signal to investors through short-term profits and dividends. Because the institutional complementarities found among LMEs require a short-term time horizon to be efficient and, therefore, most effective, this short sightedness means materialist values drive behavior in firms in these states.

In contrast, the coordinated nature of CMEs makes firms in these states more susceptible to perceptions of image or reputation and this encourages them to internalize social concerns for the environment better. Because they must satisfy a broader range of stakeholders, the institutional complementarities found among CMEs requires a longer time horizon to be effective. The result is that firms in CMEs will tend to factor stakeholder values into their business plans early on, and these norms drive the behavior of firms in these states. As a result, these factors allow CMEs to more effectively address environmental concerns.

According to the VoC approach, "in any national economy, firms will gravitate towards the mode of coordination for which there is institutional support" (Hall and Soskice 2001, 8–9). Over time, this institutional support takes on normative qualities, leading to the establishment of commonly accepted norms, rules and decision-making procedures. As a consequence, the varieties of capitalism that occur among EMEs also produce varying outcomes for environmental markets. Because firms are ultimately responsible for the majority of environmental damage, exerting governance over firms in regards to the environment requires us to understand their internal capitalist functioning. Although these speculations seem to have some support, further research in this area will be required before a more definitive explanation can be established.

C. LIMITS TO GENERALIZATION

In any type of research, it is good social scientific practice to be vigilant about overgeneralization. Hence, limits to generalization due to sample representativeness, application to other cases and research time frame will be briefly discussed as they apply to these findings.

First, in all types of research, the representativeness of the sample must be deliberated when considering its generalizability. Under even the best of circumstances, it is often difficult to study the full universe of cases reflecting every possible variation of an independent variable. In the vast majority of cases, this is not feasible, so a representative group is chosen to reflect the whole population. Although the complete universe of cases have been included in this study, with only a few exceptions due to incomplete data, some heterogeneity will inevitably result due to the differences that exist outside the economic standing of the three types of emerging markets included in my sample. In addition, these findings may be difficult to generalize to a larger set of developing economies or to make comparisons with the advanced industrialized states. However, any medium-N research should elicit some concern about the ability to safely extrapolate to a larger population and the appropriate caution should be used.

Second, due the very specific nature of the CDM market, generalizations to other environmental markets or markets in general also require some reservations. In respect to comparisons with other emissions markets, for example, it is well understood that the CDM is a very unique case. First, because the CDM is an offset market, there are distinctive limits on the states involved, making this emission market unique from the forty-four or so other carbon markets in the world today. Second, the CDM is a voluntary market that addresses the supply side of emissions reductions only. In contrast, the European Union Emissions Trading Scheme (EU ETS), the largest carbon market in the world, involves states who are required by global treaty to comply with specific caps or limits of emissions. Hence, in the EU ETS system, both the supply and demand sides are delineated and regulated. Finally, the CDM is both a climate policy and a development regime involving a range of actors. The complex nature of the CDM also makes generalization to other carbon markets difficult.

Similarly, it is very possible that the various types of capitalism will perform differently in other types of markets. In fact, I would hypothesize that financial markets will benefit from the short-term time horizons found in LMEs. In contrast, commodity markets for other common goods may benefit in ways similar to environmental markets. Research in this area must move beyond theory if it can be considered useful for effective policy development.

A final reason to be cautious about the overgeneralization of this research is due to the time frame of the study. For a variety of research agendas, time is critical as the behaviors can change yearly, monthly or even by the hour. Because the data for this research explores the formation of the CDM back in 2005, the picture presented in this research reflects a previous time period. Much has changed for many of these states. And although the types of capitalism found among the advanced industrialized economies is seen as generally static, it is not yet understood if EMEs transition through capitalist types over time as they move up the development chain. Nor is it understood how these states compare with VoCs found in the advanced economies. Time-series studies of capitalist types among the EMEs will be required to determine how they evolve. Likewise, comparisons to states with well-established VoC ideal types are necessary if we are to fully comprehend how EMEs function.

Despite these caveats, it is well understood that in all social science research, demonstrating explicit connections is a critical matter regardless of the type of causation that is explored. Although the issues associated with samples, measurement error and poor generalization illustrate some of the limitations of this study, an important baseline has been established. For example, this study has provided an empirical starting point for understanding the VoC found among the EMEs. More importantly, these findings have shed new light on how economic institutions and markets interact. This promotes improved empirical classification and aids in concept building and theory development.

9 Conclusions and Implications for Future Research

Throughout the world, environmental degradation is a growing concern. Climate change, due in large part to human activity, is now well documented. Overfishing has depleted ocean resources at a scale that may never be recovered. Biological diversity is on the decline and deforestation is at its highest levels in human history. To address these problems, an increasingly common solution is the use of market-based policies.

Throughout this book, I have explored the significance, limitations and practical implications of market-based policies within emerging economies. I conclude that although economic institutions do play a central part in determining market formation, at least in some cases, other factors also matter. For Emerging Market Economies (EMEs) in particular, other priorities such as high population levels and macroeconomic stability may also play a role. As Dani Rodrik (2011) has noted, it is not a surprise that markets require non-market institutions in order to function. "Their presence in turn begs the questions of how they are designed and whose interests they serve. When we confront these questions head on—instead of assuming them away[1]—we get a better handle on how best to design market-supporting institutions" (Rodrik 2011, 10). Understanding these economies and their competing priorities will be increasingly relevant if meaningful policy solutions are to be produced.

My research also makes clear that performance in environmental markets cannot be determined by the level of development alone. This suggests that market outcomes cannot simply be explained away by the level of development. Antiquated classifications of states are no longer helpful, and new efforts must be made to understand the economic systems found in EMEs. To address this, new theories, research methods and related typologies need to be designed and tested if we are to get a fuller understanding of how capitalism functions. Together, these efforts may help to provide new and promising insights into complex social phenomena that might otherwise be difficult to study.

A. IMPLICATIONS OF THIS RESEARCH

Scholars and policy makers alike must recognize that market development faces substantial logistical and political challenges. How can and should we use markets to solve large-scale global problems? In recognition of the complexities involved, my research has important implications for sustainable development, international policy design, global governance and the effective research methods used to understand complex social phenomena.

First, this research has important implications for sustainable economic development. It has been increasingly accepted that export promotion policies are an essential driver of growth in the developing world. Market mechanisms like the Clean Development Mechanism (CDM), and the carbon credits these projects produce, provide a means to sustain export markets while reducing the polluting effect of industrialization—but only if incentivized properly. If emerging economies are capable of skipping the mess of polluting during industrialization, then increased growth and prosperity would no longer come at a cost to the environment and human health.

In addition, policies that encourage market development have been shown to improve economic capacity in developing states. For example, China has recently announced that based on its experience with the CDM, it intends to launch a domestic cap and trade market. To maximize these benefits, a better understanding of the economic institutions within these states is required.

This research also has important implications for international policy design and implementation—especially in regards to effective market-based policies. Perhaps the most significant contribution of this research is its focus on how and why states integrate into global markets. Whereas much of the research surrounding the CDM focuses on evaluation of the established rules and regulations, my research aims to identify the causal mechanisms that drive or impede participation by EMEs. With the increasing role of market-based mechanisms, recognizing when and how market-based policies can achieve their goals is central to the international community's ability to design and implement effective policies across a range of issues.

This research also has implication for global governance. Environmental regulation is increasingly shifting to market-based regulatory mechanisms. What are the implications of their large-scale use? Research in this area could help to improve our understanding of market-based governance. For example, the protocols established in Kyoto are presently up for renewal, and thus the longer-term survival of global carbon markets is not assured. Evaluating and improving this policy option is important and timely.

Moreover, findings, like those presented in this study, illustrate new facets of global governance that may not have been considered in the past. If the evidence presented here is correct, diverse types of capitalism will require unique policies to reach common goals, such as protecting the environment or addressing the very real problem of climate change. These findings may challenge the view that global environmental problems require global solutions. Instead, policy may need to be established for various economic types—responding to their comparative strengths as a way to properly incentivize them.

In addition, research in this area has applicability beyond carbon markets to issues such as financial markets, commoditized resources (e.g. food, water and energy) and other public goods, which may not be managed properly without policies to protect them. And with time, comparisons could even be made across various types of markets. Advancing this research on market-based governance and its limitations serves to expand global governance options by allowing such work to be applied to other difficult transnational issues.

Finally, this research has implication for innovations in research methods. Although both QCA and binary logistic regression have strengths and weaknesses, neither is intrinsically superior. In fact, much of what determines their success has to do with the number of cases and causal factors, the type of data available or the type of hypotheses tested. My research has shed light on how complementary methods may be more useful, in some cases, for seeing the full picture.

In addition, understanding complex problems requires well-developed empirical approaches that allow us to consider the possibility of conjunctural causation and non-linear processes. Complex system analysis is not only about prediction, but can also be helpful to understand the behavior or underlying patterns we may encounter in our changing world. This requires scholars to consider other methods and to begin testing them in tandem with well-known, reliable approaches so that we can better understand the complex world in which we live.

B. FUTURE RESEARCH

The comparative capitalism framework uses an institutions-based approach to understand competitive matters between states. This study has benefitted from its cognitive, process-driven foundation, but the lack of overall consensus in the field has produced, at times, conflicting assumptions that have impeded the consolidation of this cumulative research paradigm. Although more recent institutional models are seen as improvements, they are in stark contrast to earlier works and create ongoing debate and confusion.

In spite of this, the comparative capitalism approach has proven fruitful as a theoretical construct for complex models of governance. However, it does not work all of the time. There are some settings in which this approach will not hold. In the study of political institutions, for example, the classic case is that of the Soviet Union at the end of the Cold War. Here, political institutions did not have meaningful or predictive value as dictated by theory. This may also be true of economic institutions, so the researcher should be aware and diligent about confirming important findings. Consequently, comparative capitalism models require more refinement, including more systematic approaches to testing—an area that should be seen as critical for future research.

Likewise, comparative capitalism research may be moving towards increased empirics, but it remains highly theoretical at the macrolevel. There is a need for more explicit empirical research surrounding coproduction and conjunctural theories like the Varieties of Capitalism. We currently lack the methodological tools for effective analysis in this area because, as Miller writes, "non-linear data is indistinguishable from random noise without a hypothesized causal model to organize it for analysis. Thus, the quantitative techniques so often used to search for meaningful patterns and eliminate untenable causal propositions in contemporary social science research cannot be used to study truly non-linear problems" (Miller 1997, 184). To make further advances, we cannot rely on models that simply throw away the anomalies and variance in the name of parsimony.

Despite some weaknesses, comparative capitalism is still a maturing research paradigm with growing potential. Institutional approaches are supportive of the trend to employ different and more demanding techniques for explicit, transparent and rigorous measurement. Although by no means pervasive, these are important developments. Determining causality can be a major intellectual challenge for future research, but these models have great potential. The better use we can make of the methodological toolbox available to us, the more accurate and reliable will be the conclusions we reach. Most importantly, this may help to encourage a more ambitious and sophisticated methodological repertoire within and across the social sciences.

NOTES

1. Adam Smith originally assumed these institutions away, claiming that governments have no place in markets (Smith 1776).

Appendix A
Operationalization of the Variables

This appendix establishes the protocol for the operationalization of the independent variables for this research.

A. INDEPENDENT VARIABLES

To operationalize the independent variables for this project, a protocol has been established for each of the Varieties of Capitalism (VoC) and control variables. Each variable is composed of two to five underlying subindicators. Indicators are chosen because they are the best available measures for the characteristics outlined in the VoC literature. Every subindicator contributes equally to its parent category and every category contributes equally to the overall outcome for each case. The proposed indicators are measured using either survey or quantitative data and then scaled from 1–7, to keep them in line with the data scale used by the World Economic Forum. For the VoC variables only, a higher score is correlated to a Liberal Market Economy (LME) ideal type. In contrast, lower scores are correlated to a Controlled Market Economy (CME) ideal type.

VoC 1: Labor Relations

Centralized (CME) or Decentralized (LME) labor relations:

- Centralized systems, found in CMEs, generally have strong unions or other collective bargaining institutions for labor. They also include high levels of employment protection such as employment compensation, regulated income equality and mandatory contract lengths. As a result, labor relations are less flexible and highly regulated.
- Decentralized systems, found in LMEs, have weak to no employment protection regulations, less generous unemployment benefits and little or no institutions for workforce participation, firm-level collective bargaining or individualized labor contracts (Hall and Soskice 2001, 21–33).

Proposed Indicators

1. *Cooperation in labor-employer relations*
   - *1 = cooperative; 7 = confrontational*
2. *Flexibility of wage determination*
   - *1=by centralized bargaining process; 7 = up to each individual company*
3. *Hiring and firing practices*
   - *1=highly regulated; 7 = flexibly determined by employers*
4. *Redundancy or "layoff" costs, in weeks of salary*
   - *1 = high levels; 7 = low levels*

Together, these subindicators are combined to operationalize the independent variable for labor relations. For this, cluster analysis identifies sixteen Centralized (CME) cases and fifteen Decentralized (LME) cases.

VoC 2: Finance

Bank-based (CME) or Market-based (LME) financing:

- Countries with bank-based financing source capital through domestic banks that monitor and maintain proper liquidity and risk levels. High domestic savings rates often mean less Foreign Direct Investment (FDI) and slower innovation, but greater stability.
- Countries with capital market-based financing are able to efficiently source capital directly to borrowers through securities markets. They often have easier access to loans and higher levels of venture capital that help to spur innovation.

Proposed Indicators

1. *Relative size of local equity markets*
   - *1 = not efficient; 7 = very efficient*
2. *Ease of access to loans*
   - *1 = very difficult; 7 = very easy*
3. *Venture capital availability*
   - *1 = very difficult; 7 = very easy*
4. *Stock market capitalization*
   - *Market value of listed domestic companies as a percentage of Gross Domestic Product (GDP)*
   - *1 = low capitalization; 7 = high capitalization*

These subindicators are combined to operationalize the independent variable for finance. Here, cluster analysis produces nineteen Bank-based (CME) cases and twelve Market-based (LME) cases.

VoC 3: Inter-Firm Relations

Obligatory (CME) or Competitive (LME) inter-firm relations:

- States where inter-firm relations are obligatory tend to have increased cooperation among firms and suppliers, a focus on specific goods production and a greater number of industry associations.
- States where inter-firm relations are competitive tend to have greater levels of private R&D, a focus on services and general goods production, strong intellectual property rights and reduced intra-industry cooperation.

Proposed Indicators[1]

1. *Nature of competitive advantage for domestic companies*
   - *1 = low-cost or natural resources; 7 = unique products and processes*
2. *In your country, how sophisticated are production processes?*
   - *1 = not at all—labor-intensive methods or previous generations of process technology prevail; 7 = highly—the world's best and most efficient process technology prevails*
3. *Do exporting companies have a narrow or broad presence in the value chain?*
   - *1 = narrow, primarily involved in individual steps of the value chain; 7 = broad, present across the entire value chain*
4. *Quality of Local supplier networks*
   - *1 = very poor; 7 = very good*

Together, these subindicators are combined to operationalize the independent variable for inter-firm relations. Cluster analysis suggests thirteen Obligatory (CME) and eighteen Competitive (LME) cases.

VoC 4: Education and Vocational Training

Specific Skills (CME) or General Skills (LME) in education and vocational training:

- Countries with specific skills tend to privilege those workers with well-refined, but nontransferable skills (e.g. artisans, technicians). This produces long-term, nontransferable skills and lower general literacy levels. Training for jobs is often done in the work place or through apprenticeships.
- Countries with general labor skills tend to privilege those workers with developed and portable skills. Compulsory education requirements in these states produce a society with a general skill base and broad literacy levels. Training for jobs is generally done through colleges and universities.

Proposed Indicators

1. *Tertiary education (e.g. post-secondary education) enrollment rate*
   - *Gross tertiary education enrollment rate*
   - *1 = low; 7 = high*
2. *Quality of education system*
   - *Q: How well does the educational system in your country meet the needs of a competitive economy?*
   - *1 = not well at all; 7 = very well*
3. *Quality of management schools*
   - *1 = poor; 7 = excellent—among the best in the world*
4. *Extent of staff training*
   - *Q: To what extent do companies in your country invest in training and employee development?*
   - *1 = to a great extent; 7 = hardly at all*

Together, these subindicators are combined to operationalize the independent variable for education and vocational training. Cluster analysis produces sixteen Specific Skills (CME) cases and fifteen General Skills (LME) cases.

VoC 5: Corporate Governance

Dispersed (CME) or Concentrated (LME) corporate governance:

- Countries with dispersed ownership structures (e.g. dispersed market control) generally use consensus management and insider control across a wide range of agents and have higher levels of organized labor. Ownership is dispersed among a wide range of shareholders and institutional investors.
- Countries with concentrated ownership structures use management-based decision making that is greatly influenced by shareholder influence. Ownership is concentrated among large block holders, such as families, banks and corporations and lower levels of organized labor are common.

Proposed Indicators

1. *How would you characterize corporate governance by investors and boards of directors in your country?*
   - *1 = management has little accountability to investors and boards; 7 = investors and boards exert strong supervision of management decisions*
2. *Protection of minority shareholders' interests*
   - *1 = not protected at all; 7 = fully protected*

3. *Strength of investor protections*
   - *Strength of Investor Protection Index on a 0–10 (best) scale (World Bank 2012)*

Together, these subindicators are combined to operationalize the independent variable for corporate governance. Cluster analysis identifies twelve Dispersed (CME) cases and eighteen Concentrated (LME) cases. Note: The case of Tunisia lacks sufficient data to be analyzed across all three measures. Using missing data estimation techniques, Tunisia was assigned to the LME category.

B. CONTROL VARIABLES

CON 1: Macroeconomic Stability: Stable or Unstable

Proposed Indicators

1. *Country credit rating*[2]
   - *Expert assessment of the probability of sovereign debt default on a 0–100 scale*
2. *Annual inflation rate*
   - *Annual percent change in year average consumer price index*
3. *Government budget*[3]
   - *General government budget balance as a percentage of GDP*
4. *General government debt level*
   - *Gross general government debt as a percentage of GDP*

Together, these subindicators are combined to operationalize the control variable for macroeconomic stability. Cluster analysis produces twelve Stable cases and nineteen Unstable cases.

CON2: Infrastructure: Developed or Underdeveloped

Proposed Indicators

1. *Quality of overall infrastructure (e.g., transport, telephony and energy)*
   - *1 = extremely underdeveloped; 7 = extensive and efficient by international standards*
2. *Quality of roads*
   - *1 = extremely underdeveloped; 7 = extensive and efficient by international standards*
3. *Quality of railway infrastructure*
   - *1 = extremely underdeveloped; 7 = extensive and efficient by international standards*
4. *Quality of port infrastructure*
   - *1 = extremely underdeveloped; 7 = well developed and efficient by international standards*

5. *Quality of electricity supply (e.g. lack of interruptions and lack of voltage fluctuations)*
   - *1 = insufficient and suffers frequent interruptions; 7 = sufficient and reliable*

Together, these sub-indicators are combined to operationalize the control variable for infrastructure. Cluster analysis identifies eleven Developed cases and twenty Underdeveloped cases.

CON 3: Public Institutions: Reliable or Unreliable

Proposed Indicators

1. *Public trust in politicians*
   - *1 = very low; 7 = very high*
2. *Irregular payment and bribes*
   - *Q: In your country, how common is it for firms to make undocumented extra payments or bribes connected with (a) imports and exports; (b) public utilities; (c) annual tax payments; (d) awarding of public contracts and licenses; (e) obtaining favorable judicial decisions?*
   - *1 = very common; 7 = never occurs*
3. *Transparency of government policymaking*
   - *Q: How easy is it for businesses in your country to obtain information about changes in government policies and regulations affecting their activities?*
   - *1 = impossible; 7 = extremely easy*
4. *Wasteful government spending*
   - *Q: How would you rate the composition of public spending in your country?*
   - *1 = extremely wasteful; 7 = highly efficient in providing necessary goods/services*
5. *Business cost of crime and violence*
   - *Q: To what extent does the incidence of crime and violence impose costs on businesses in your country?*
   - *1 = to a great extent; 7 = not at all*

Together, these subindicators are combined to operationalize the control variable for public institutions. Cluster analysis produces fourteen Reliable cases and seventeen Unreliable cases.

CON 4: Population: High or Low

Proposed Indicator

1. *Population*
   - *Total population in millions (UN, 2011/2012)*
   - *1 = low population; 7 = high population*

Together, these subindicators are combined to operationalize the control variable for population. The final outcome is analyzed using cluster analysis to produce two high population cases and twenty-nine low population cases.

NOTES

1. These indicators have been inverted from their original scale. In other words, the scale presented (1–7) has been inverted from the original survey questions to reflect the VoC characteristic reflected in the index variables in my dataset. Although this is not required, it was undertaken for consistency and to prevent confusion.
2. Institutional Investor's Country Credit ratings are based on information provided by senior economists and sovereign-debt analysts at leading global banks and money management firms. Twice a year, the respondents grade each country on a scale of 0 to 100, with 100 representing the least chance of default.
3. Net lending (+)/ borrowing (–) is calculated as general government revenue minus total expenditure. This measures the extent to which the general government is either putting financial resources at the disposal of other sectors in the economy and nonresidents (net lending), or utilizing the financial resources generated by other sectors and nonresidents (net borrowing). This balance is an indicator of the financial impact of general government activity on the rest of the economy and nonresidents (IMF 2012).

References

Ahrens, Joachim and Patrick Jünemann. 2007. "Transitional Institutions, Institutional Complementarities and Economic Performance in China." *Duisburger Arbeitspapiere zur Ostasienwirtschaft* 72.

Albert, Michael. 1991. *Capitalism vs. Capitalism: How America's Obsession with Individual Achievement and Short-term Profit Has Led It to the Brink of Collapse.* New York: Four Walls Eight Windows.

Alyanak, Leyla. 2009. "Population Dynamics and Climate Change." Presented at the United Nations Population Fund Conference on Climate and People, 23–24 March.

Amable, Bruno. 2003. *The Diversity of Modern Capitalism.* Oxford: Oxford University Press.

Andriesse, Edo. [2006] 2008. *Regional Varieties of Capitalism: Inter-firm Relations and Access to Finance in Satun (Thailand) and Perlis (Malaysia).* Rotterdam: Institute of Social Studies of Erasmus University Rotterdam (ISS), ISS Working Papers–General Series #19192.

Andriesse, Edo and Guus van Westen. 2009. "Unsustainable Varieties of Capitalism along the Thailand–Malaysia Border? The Role of Institutional Complementarities in Regional Development." *Asia Pacific Journal of Management* 26(3): 459–479.

Arrow, Kenneth, Bert Bolin, Robert Costanza, Partha Dasgupta, Carl Folke, C. S. Holling, Bengt-Owe. Jansson, Simon Levin, Karl-Goran. Mäler, Charles Perrings and David Pimentel. 1995. "Economic Growth, Carrying Capacity, and the Environment." *Science* 268: 520–521.

Battig, Michèle and Thomas Bernauer. 2009. "National Institutions and Global Public Goods: Are Democracies More Cooperative in Climate Change Policy?" *International Organization* 63: 281–308.

Becht, Marco and Alisa. Roel. 1999. "Blockholding in Europe: An International Comparison." *European Economic Review* 43: 1049–1056.

Benecke, Gudrun. 2009. "Varieties of Carbon Governance: Taking Stock of the Local Carbon Market in India." *The Journal of Environment & Development* 18(4) (December): 346–370.

Benney, Tabitha. 2011. "Embedded Approaches to Governing Climate Change." Presented at the International Studies Association Annual Conference, Montreal, Canada.

Berger, Suzanne and Ronald Philip Dore. 1996. *National Diversity and Global Capitalism.* Ithaca: Cornell University Press.

Betsill, Michele and Matthew Hoffmann. 2011. "The Contours of 'Cap and Trade': The Evolution of Emissions Trading Systems for Greenhouse Gases." *Review of Policy Research* 28 (1): 83–106.

Blair, Margaret and Mark Roe. 1999. *Employees and Corporate Governance*. Washington: Brookings Institution Press.

Boole, George. 1847. *The Mathematical Analysis of Logic: Being an Essay Towards the Calculus of Deductive Reasoning*. Oxford: Basil Blackwell.

Borensztein, Eduardo, Josède Gregorioand and Jong-Wha Lee. 1998. "How Does Foreign Direct Investment Affect Economic Growth?" *Journal of International Economics* (45): 115–135.

Brady, Henry E. and David Collier. 2004. *Rethinking Social Inquiry: Diverse Tools, Shared Standards*. Lanham: Rowman & Littlefield.

Buchen, Clemens. 2004. What Kind of Capitalism Is Emerging in Eastern Europe? Varieties of Capitalism in Estonia and Slovenia. Managing the Economic Transition, University of Cambridge.

Butzengeiger-Geyer, Sonja, Axel Michaelowa, Michel Köhler and Martin Stadelmann. 2011. "Market Mechanisms for Adaptation to Climate –Change—Lessons from Mitigation and a Pathway to Implementation." Zurich: Center for Comparative International Studies.

Carney, Michael, Eric Gedajlovic and Xiaohua Yang. 2009. "Varieties of Asian Capitalism: Toward an Institutional Theory of Asian Enterprise." *Asia Pacific Journal of Management* 26(3): 361–380.

Casey, Terrance. 2007. "Is Britain a Liberal Economy? British Capitalism in Comparative Perspective," Paper presented at the 2007 American Political Science Association Conference in Chicago, IL.

CDM Executive Board. 2011. *Climate Change, Carbon Markets and the CDM: A Call to Action*. Luxembourg: CDM Policy Dialogue. ISBN: 92-9219-100-4 (www.cdmpolicydialogue.org).

Chand, Satish, Ron Duncan and Doan Quang. 2001. "The Role of Institutions in the Development of Vietnam." *ASEAN Economic Bulletin* 18(3): 276–288.

Chang, Ha-Joon. 2003. *Restructuring Korea Inc.: Financial Crisis, Corporate Reform, and Institutional Transition*. London: Routledge.

Chasek, Pamela S., Downie, David Leonard and Janet Welsh Brown. 2014. *Global Environmental Politics*. Boulder: Westview Press, Sixth Edition.

Christoff, Peter and Robyn Eckersely. 2011. "Comparing State Responses." In *The Oxford Handbook of Climate Change and Society*, eds. John S. Dryzek, Richard B. Norgaard, and David Schlosberg. Oxford: Oxford University Press, 431–448.

Clark, William R., Michael J. Gilligan, and Matt Golder. 2006. "A Simple Multivariate Test for Asymmetric Hypotheses." *Political Analysis* 14(3): 311–331.

Coates, David. 2002. *Varieties of Capitalism, Varieties of Approaches*. New York: Palgrave Macmillan.

Cohen, Benjamin J. 2009. "Toward a Leaderless Currency World." In *The Future of the Dollar*, eds. Eric Helleiner and J. Kirshner. Ithaca: Cornell University Press, 142–163.

Congleton, Roger D. 1992. "Political Institutions and Pollution Control." *Review of Economics and Statistics* 74(3):412–421.

Copi, Irving M., Carl Cohen, and K. D. McMahon. 2011. *Introduction to Logic*. Upper Saddle River, NJ: Pearson Education.

Crouch, Colin. 2005. *Capitalist Diversity and Change: Recombinant Governance and Institutional Entrepreneurs*. Oxford: Oxford University Press.

Crouch, Colin and William Streeck. 1997. *Political Economy of Modern Capitalism: Mapping Convergence and Diversity*. London: Sage.

Currana, M. Martin and Dominic Moranb. 2006. "Impact of the FTSE Goods Index on Firm Price: An Event Study." *Journal of Environmental Management* 82(March): 529–537.

Dales, John H. 1968. *Pollution, Property and Prices*. Toronto: University of Toronto Press.

De Meur, Gisèle and Benoît Rihoux. 2002. *The Analysis of Qualitative-Quantitative Comparison: Approaches, Techniques and Applications in the Social Sciences*. Louvain-la-Neuve, Belgium: Academia-Bruylant.

Dechezlepretre, Antoine, Matthieu Glachant and Yann Menier. 2009. "Technology Transfer by CDM Projects: A Comparison of Brazil, China, India, and Mexico." *Energy Policy* 37: 703–711.

Deeg, Richard. 1999. "The German State Banks: Global Players in International Financial Markets." *Journal of Comparative Economics* 29: 195–197.

Dietz, Thomas, Amy Fitzgerald and Rachael Shwom. 2005. "Environmental Values." *Annual Review of Environmental Resources* 30: 335–372.

DiMaggio, Paul and Walter W. Powell. 1983. *The Iron Cage Revisited: Conformity and Diversity in Organizational Fields*. New Haven, CT: Institution for Social and Policy Studies, Yale University.

Dobbin, Frank. 1994. *Forging Industrial Policy: The United States, Britain, and France in the Railway Age*. Cambridge: Cambridge University Press.

Dodgson, Mark. 2009. "Asia's National Innovation Systems: Institutional Adaptability and Rigidity in the Face of Global Innovation Challenges." *Asia Pacific Journal of Management* 26(3): 589–609.

Dore, Ronald. 1986. *Flexible Rigidities: Industrial Policy and Structural Adjustment in the Japanese Economy 1970–80*. London: The Athlone Press.

Dore, Ronald. 2000. *Stock Market Capitalism-Welfare Capitalism: Japan and Germany versus the Anglo-Saxons*. Oxford: Oxford University Press

Easterly, William. 2006. "Reliving the '50s: The Big Push, Poverty Traps, and Takeoffs in Economic Development." *Journal of Economic Growth* 11(4): 289–318.

Ebenau, Matthias M. 2012. "Varieties of Capitalism or Dependency? A Critique of the VOC Approach for Latin America." *Competition and Change* 16(3): 206–223.

Eckersley, Robyn. 2004. *The Green State: Rethinking Democracy and Sovereignty*. Cambridge, MA: MIT Press.

The Economist. 2008. "Ins and Outs: Acronyms BRIC Out All Over" *The Economist*. (Sept 18). (www.economist.com/node/12080703).

Edwards, Jeremy and Klaus Fischer. 1994. *Banks, Finance and Investment in Germany*. Cambridge: Cambridge University Press.

Engel, Anita, Lisa Knoll, and Huth Martin. 2008. "Preparing for the 'Real' Market: National Patterns of Institutional Learning and Company Behavior in the European Emissions Trading Scheme (EU ETS)," *European Environment*. 18(5): 276–297.

Enkvist, Per-Anders, Jens Dinkel and Charles Lin. 2010. *Impact of the Financial Crisis on Carbon Economics: Version 2.1 of the Global Greenhouse Gas Abatement Cost Curve Report*. McKinsey and Company www.mckinsey.com/clientservice/sustainability/pdf/Impact_Financial_Crisis_Carbon_Economics_GHGcostcurveV2.1.pdf.).

Estévez-Abe, Margarita, Torben Iversen and David Soskice. 2001. "Social Protection and the Formation of Skills: A Reinterpretation of the Welfare State." In *Varieties of Capitalism: The Institutional Foundations of Comparative Advantage*, eds. Peter Hall and David Soskice. Oxford: Oxford University Press, 145–183.

Esty, Daniel and Michael E. Porter. 2005. "National Environmental Performance: An Empirical Analysis of Policy Results and Determinates." *Environment and Development Economics* 10: 391–434.

Evans, Peter. 1995. *Embedded Autonomy: States and Industrial Transformation*. Princeton, NJ: Princeton University Press.

Feldmann, Magnus. 2006. "Emerging Varieties of Capitalism in Transition Countries: Industrial Relations and Wage Bargaining in Estonia and Slovenia." *Comparative Political Studies* 39(7): 829–854.

Fitzroy, Felix R. and Kornelius Kraft. 2005. "Co-determination, Efficiency and Productivity." *British Journal of Industrial Relations* 43(June): 233–247.

Fligstein, Neil. 2002. *The Architecture of Markets: An Economic Sociology of Twenty-First-Century Capitalist Societies*. Princeton: Princeton University Press.

Fligstein, Neil and Jianjun Zhang. 2011. "A New Agenda for Research on the Trajectory of Chinese Capitalism." *Management and Organization Review* 7: 39–62.

Foran, John. 2005. *Taking Power: On the Origins of Third World Revolutions*. Cambridge: Cambridge University Press.

Friberg, Lars. 2009. "Varieties of Carbon Governance: The Clean Development Mechanism in Brazil—a Success Story Challenged." *The Journal of Environment & Development* 18:4 (December): 395–424.

Frognier, André-Paul. 2002. "Forward." In *The Analysis of Qualitative-Quantitative Comparison: Approaches, Techniques and Applications in the Social Sciences*, eds. G. De Meur and B. Rihoux. Louvain-la-Neuve, Belgium: Academia-Bruylant.

FTSE Group. 2012. "Country Classification in FTSE Global Benchmarks" *FTSE Indices*. (www.ftse.com/Indices/Country_Classification/index.jsp).

Fuhr, Harald and Markus Lederer. 2009. "Varieties of Carbon Governance in Newly Industrializing Countries." *The Journal of Environment & Development* 18:4 (December): 327–345.

Gallagher, Kelly Sims and Joanna Lewis. 2012. "China's Quest for a Green Economy." In *Environmental Policy*, 8th Edition, eds. Norman Vig and Michael Kraft. Washington, DC: CQ Press.

Gillenwater, Michael and Stephen Seres. 2011. *Clean Development Mechanism: A Review of the First International Offset Program*. Arlington: Center for Climate and Energy Solutions. (www.issuelab.org/permalink/resource/12681).

Gingerich, Daniel and Peter Hall. 2004. "Varieties of Capitalism and Institutional Complementarities in the Macroeconomy: An Empirical Assessment." *Berlin Journal of Sociology* 1(2004): 5–32.

Gleditsch, Nils and Bjorn Sverdrup. 2003. "Democracy and the Environment." In *Human Security and the Environment: International Comparisons*, eds. E.A. Page and M. Redclift. Cheltenham: Edward Elgar:45–70.

Goertz, Gary. 2006. "Introduction to the Special Issue: Causal Complexity and Qualitative Methods." *Political Analysis* 14(3):223–226.

Granovetter, Mark. 1985. "Economic Action and Social Structure: The Problem of Embeddedness." *American Journal of Sociology* 91(3): 481–510.

Green, Andy, John Preston and Jan G. Janmaat. 2006. *Education, Equality and Social Cohesion*. New York: Palgrave Macmillan.

Green, Andy, Tarek Mostafa and John Preston. 2010. "The Chimera of Competitiveness: Varieties of Capitalism and the Economic Crisis." *LLAKES Research Paper (8)*. Centre for Learning and Life Chances in Knowledge Economies and Societies, Institute of Education, University of London, London.

Grofman, Bernard and Carsten Q. Schneider. 2009. "An Introduction to Crisp Set QCA, with a Comparison to Binary Logistic Regression." *Political Research Quarterly* 62(December): 662–672.

Guagnano, Gregory A., Paul C. Stern and Thomas Dietz. 1995. "Influences on Attitude-Behavior Relationships A Natural Experiment with Curbside Recycling." *Environment and Behavior*. (September) 27: 5, 699–718.

Haggard, Stephan. 1990. *Pathways from the Periphery: The Politics of Growth in Newly Industrializing Countries*. Ithaca, NY: Cornell University Press.

Hall, Peter A. and David Soskice. 2001. *Varieties of Capitalism: The Institutional Foundations of Comparative Advantage*. Oxford: Oxford University Press.

Hall, Peter and Rosemary Taylor. 1996. "Political Science and the Three New Institutionalisms." *Political Studies* 44: 936–957.

Hancke, Bob. 2009. *Debating Varieties of Capitalism*. Oxford: Oxford University Press.

Hancke, Bob, Martin Rhodes and Mark Thatcher. 2009. "Beyond Varieties of Capitalism." In *Debating Varieties of Capitalism*, ed. Bob Hancke. Oxford: Oxford University Press, 273–300.

Hardee, Karen and Leiwen Jiang. 2009. *How Do Recent Population Trends Matter to Climate Change?* Washington: Population Action International. www.issuelab.org/permalink/resource/3174).

Hardin, Garrett. 1968. "The Tragedy of the Commons." *Science* 162 (December): 1243–1248.

Hart, Jeffrey. 1992. *Rival Capitalists: International Competitiveness in the United States, Japan, and Western Europe*. Ithaca: Cornell University Press.

Hellström, Johan. 2011. "Conditional Hypotheses in Comparative Social Science: Mixed-Method Approaches to Middle-Sized Data Analysis" *Methodological Innovations Online* 6(2): 71–102.

Heugens, Pursey P. M. A. R., Marc van Essen, Marc and J. (Hans) van Oosterhout. 2009. "Meta-analyzing Ownership Concentration and Firm Performance in Asia: Towards a More Fine-grained Understanding." *Asia Pacific Journal of Management* 26(3): 481–512.

Hoffmann, Matthew J. 2003. "Constructing a Complex World: The Frontiers of International Relations Theory and Foreign Policy Making." *Asian Journal of Political Science* 11(January): 37–57.

Hollingsworth, J. Rogers and Robert Boyer. 1997. *Contemporary Capitalism: The Embeddedness of Institutions*. Cambridge: Cambridge University Press.

Hollingsworth, J. Rogers, Philippe C. Schmitter and Wolfgang Streeck. 1994. *Governing Capitalist Economies*. Oxford: Oxford University Press.

Hutton, Will. 1995. *The State We're In*. Kent: Mackays of Chattam.

Hutton, Will. 1999. *The State to Come*. London: Vintage.

Hutton, Will. 2002. *The World We're In*. London: Little and Brown.

Ignatow, Gabe. 2011. "What Has Globalization Done to Developing Countries' Public Libraries?" *International Sociology* 26(6): 746–768.

International Labour Organization. 2010. *ILOSTAT Database*. Gene've, Switzerland: International Labour Organisation.

International Monetary Fund (IMF). 2012. *World Economic Outlook: A Survey*. Washington, DC: International Monetary Fund.

Jackson, Gregory and Richard Deeg. 2006. *How Many Varieties of Capitalism? Comparing the Comparative Institutional Analyses of Capitalist Diversity*. Colonge: Max-Planck-Institute.

Jackson, Gregory and Sigurt Vitols. 2001. "Between Financial Commitment, Market Liquidity and Corporate Governance: Occupational Pensions in Britain, Germany, Japan and the USA." In *Comparing Welfare Capitalism: Social Policy and Political Economy in Europe, Japan and the USA*, ed. Bernhard Ebbinghaus and Philip Manow. London: Routledge, 171–189.

Kang, Myung-koo. 2008. "The Varieties of Capitalism in East Asia: Politics of Economic Reforms." Course Syllabus. Stanford University.

Kasteng, Jonas, Arne Karlsson and Carina Lindberg. 2004. *Differentiation Between Developing Countries in the WTO*. Jönköping: Swedish Board of Agriculture.

Katz, Aaron, Matthias vom Hau and James Mahoney. 2005. "Explaining the Great Reversal in Spanish America." *Sociological Methods & Research* 33(4): 539–573.

Katzenstein, Peter J. 1974. *Corporatism and Change: Austria, Switzerland, and the Politics of Industry*. Ithaca: Cornell University Press.

Katzenstein, Peter J. 1985. *Small States in World Markets: Industrial Policy in Europe*. Ithaca: Cornell University Press.

Keohane, Nathaniel O. and Sheila M. Olmstead. 2007. *Markets and the Environment*. Washington, DC: Island Press.

King, Gary, Robert O. Keohane and Sidney Verba. 1994. *Designing Social Inquiry: Scientific Inference in Qualitative Research*. Princeton: Princeton University Press.

Knox-Hayes, Janelle. 2009. "The Developing Carbon Financial Service Industry: Expertise, Adaptation and Complementarity in London and New York." *Journal of Economic Geography* 9 (6): 749–777.

Knox-Hayes, Janelle. 2010. "Creating the Carbon Market Institution: Analysis of the Organizations and Relationships That Build the Market." *Competition and Change* 14(3–4): 176–202.

Kuznets, Simon (1955). "Economic Growth and Income Inequality." *American Economic Review* 49: 1–28.

Lane, David Stuart and Matin R. Myant. 2007. *Varieties of Capitalism in Post-Communist Countries*. Basingstoke, UK: Palgrave Macmillan.

Lauder, Hugh, Phillip Brown and David Ashton. 2008. "Globalization, Skill Formation and the Varieties of Capitalism Approach." *New Political Economy* 13(1): 19–35.

Lazonick, William. 1992. *Organization and Technology in Capitalist Development*. Aldershot, UK: Edward Elgar.

Lazonick, William and Mary O'Sullivan. 2002. *Corporate Governance and Sustainable Prosperity*. Basingstoke, UK: Palgrave.

Levin, Peter and Wendy N. Espeland. 2002. "Pollution Futures: Commensuration Commodification and the Market for Air." In *Organizations, Policy, and the Natural Environment: Institutional and Strategic Perspectives*, eds. Andrew J. Hoffman and M. J. Ventresca. Stanford: Stanford University Press, 119–147.

Li, Quan and Rafael Reuveny. 2006. "Democracy and Environmental Degradation." *International Studies Quarterly* 50: 935–956.

Long, J.S. 1997. *Regression Models for Categorical and Limited Dependent Variables*. Thousand Oaks, CA: Sage Publications.

Lottes, Ilsa L. 1996. "Using and Interpreting Logistic Regression: A Guide for Teachers and Students." *Teaching Sociology* 24(3):284–98.

Lucas, Robert E. B., David Wheeler and Hemamala Hettige. 1992. "Economic Development, Environmental Regulation and the International Migration of Toxic Industrial Pollution: 1960–1988." In *International Trade and the Environment*, World Bank Discussion Paper No. 159, Washington, DC: World Bank.

McKenzie, Donald. 2009. "Making Things the Same: Gases, Emission Rights and the Politics of Carbon Markets." *Accounting, Organizations and Society* 34(3–4): 440–455.

Maher, Maria and Thomas Andersson. 1999. *Corporate Governance: Effects on Firm Performance and Economic Growth*. Paris: Organization for Economic Co-operation and Development.

Mase, Bryan. 2007. "The Impact of Changes in the FTSE 100 Index." *Financial Review* 42(August): 461–484.

MasterCard. 2011. *Emerging Markets Index Website*. (http://insights.mastercard.com/).

Midlarsky, Manus I. 1998. "Democracy and the Environment: An Empirical Assessment." *Journal of Peace Research* 35(3): 341–361.

Mikler, John. 2011. "Plus ça Change? A Varieties of Capitalism Approach to Social Concern for the Environment." *Global Society* 25(3): 331–352.

Mikler, John, and Neil E. Harrison. 2012. "Varieties of Capitalism and Technological Innovation for Climate Change Mitigation." *New Political Economy* 17(2): 179–208.

Mill, John Stuart Mill. 1843/2009. *A System of Logic, Vol. 1*. Echo, OR: Echo Library.

Mill, John Stuart. 1848. *Principles of Political Economy*. Alexandria: Library of Alexandria.

Miller, Clark, Sheila Jasanoff, Marybeth Long, William Clark, Nancy Dickson, Alastair Iles, and Tom Parris. 1997. "Shaping Knowledge, Defining Uncertainty:

The Dynamic Role of Assessments." In *Global Environmental Assessment Team*, ed. Clark Miller. Calverton, MD: IGES/CARE. (http://grads.iges.org/geaproject1997/gea4.html).

Mills, Julianne H. and Thomas A Waite. 2009. "Economic Prosperity, Biodiversity Conservation, and the Environmental Kuznets Curve." *Ecological Economics* 68 (7): 2087–2095.

Mitchell, Ronald. 2009. "The Influence of International Institutions: Institutional Design, Compliance, Effectiveness, and Endogeneity." in *Power, Interdependence, and Nonstate Actors in World Politics*, eds. Helen V. Milner and Andrew Moravcsik. Princeton, NJ: Princeton University Press, 66–85.

Moser, Caroline O. N., and David Satterthwaite. 2008. *Towards Pro-Poor Adaptation to Climate Change in the Urban Centres of Low- and Middle-Income Countries*. London: IIED.

Mykhnenko, Vlad. 2007. "Strengths and Weaknesses of 'Weak Co-ordination: Economic Institutions, Revealed Comparative Advantages, and Socio-Economic Performance of Mixed Market Economies in Poland and Ukraine'.' In *Beyond Varieties of Capitalism: Conflict, Contradictions and Complementarities in the European Economy*, eds. Bob Hancké, Martin Rhodes, and Mark Thatcher. Oxford: Oxford University Press.

Neumayer, Eric. 2002. "Do Democracies Exhibit Stronger International Environmental Commitment?" *Journal of Peace Research* 39(2): 139–164.

Newell, Peter. 2009. "Varieties of CDM Governance: Some Reflections." *The Journal of Environment & Development* 18:4 (December): 425–435.

Noble, Gregory W. 2005. "Globalization Meets Coordinated Capitalism in the Japanese and Korean Auto Industries." Presented at the American Sociological Association Annual Meeting, Washington, DC.

North, Douglass C. 1990. *Institutions, Institutional Change and Economic Performance*. Cambridge: Cambridge University Press.

Organization of Economic Development and Cooperation. 2000. *Designing the Clean Development Mechanism: Operational and Institutional Issues*. Paris, France: Organization for Economic Co-operation and Development.

Orru, Marco, Nicole W. Biggart and Gary G. Hamilton, 1997. *The Economic Organization of East Asian Capitalism*. Thousand Oaks, CA: Sage.

Ostrom, Elinor. 2007. "A Diagnostic Approach for Going Beyond Panaceas." *Proceedings of The National Academy of Sciences* 104(39): 15181–15187.

Panayotou, Theodore. 1993. *Empirical Tests and Policy Analysis of Environmental Degradation at Different Stages of Economic Development*. Working Paper WP238, Technology and Employment Programme, International Labour Office, Geneva.

Peck, Jamie and Jun Zhang. 2013. "A Variety of Capitalism . . . with Chinese Characteristics?" *Journal of Economic Geography* 13(3): 357–396.

Perman, Roger and David I. Stern. 2003. "Evidence from Panel Unit Root and Cointegration Tests That the Environmental Kuznets Curve Does Not Exist." *Australian Journal of Agricultural and Resource Economics*, 47(3): 325–347.

Phillips, Nicola. 2004. *The Southern Cone Model: The Political Economy of Regional Capitalist Development in Latin America*. London: Routledge.

Pigou, Arthur Cecil. 1920. *The Economics of Welfare*. London: Macmillan and Company.

Piore, Michael J., and Charles F. Sabel. 1984. *The Second Industrial Divide: Possibilities for Prosperity*. New York: Basic Books.

Polanyi, Karl. 1946. *The Great Transformation: The Political and Economic Origins of Our Time*. Boston, MA: Beacon Press.

Pontusson, Jonas. 2005. *Inequality and Prosperity: Social Europe vs. Liberal America*. Ithaca, NY: Cornell University Press.

Porter, Michael E., Klaus Schwab and Augusto López-Claros. 2006. *The Global Competitiveness Report 2006–2007*. Basingstoke: Palgrave Macmillan.

Pulver, Simone. 2011. "Corporate Responses." In *Oxford Handbook on Climate and Society*, eds. John Dryzek and Richard Norgaard. Oxford: Oxford University Press, 581–593.

Pulver, Simone. 2013. "A Climate Leader? The Politics and Practice of Climate Governance in Mexico" In *Climate Governance in the Developing World*, eds. David Held, Charles Roger and Eva-Maria Nag. Cambridge: Polity Press, 174–197.

Quine, Willard V. 1952. "The Problem of Simplifying Truth Functions." *American Mathematical Monthly* 59:521–531.

Radice, Henry. 2000. "Globalization and National Capitalisms: Theorizing Convergence and Differentiation." *Review of International Political Economy* 7(4): 719–742

Ragin, Charles C. 1987. *The Comparative Method: Moving Beyond Qualitative and Quantitative Strategies*. Thousand Oaks, CA: University of California Press.

Ragin, Charles C. 1997. "Current Issues in Comparative Macrosociology: A Debate on Methodological Issues." In *Methodological Issues in Comparative Social Research*, ed Lars Mjøset. Greenwich: JAI Press, 27–42.

Ragin, Charles C. 2000. *Fuzzy-Set Social Science*. Chicago: University of Chicago Press.

Ragin, Charles C. 2008. *Redesigning Social Inquiry: Fuzzy Sets and Beyond*. Chicago: University of Chicago Press.

Ragin, Charles C., Kriss A. Drass and Sean Davey. 2006. *Fuzzy-Set/Qualitative Comparative Analysis 2.0*. Tucson: University of Arizona.

Rangone, Marco and Stefano Solari. 2009. "Southern European Capitalism and the Social Costs of Business Enterprise." Presented at the SASE Annual Conference, Paris, France.

Redding, Gordon and Michael A.Witt. "China's Business System and Its Future Trajectory." *Asia Pacific Journal of Management* 26(3): 381–399.

Ricardo, David. 1966. *Economic Essays*. New York: A.M. Kelley.

Rihoux, Benoît and Charles C. Ragin. 2009. *Configurational Comparative Methods: Qualitative Comparative Analysis (QCA) and Related Techniques*. Thousand Oaks: Sage.

Ritchie, Bryan K. 2009. "Economic Upgrading in a State-coordinated, Liberal Market Economy." *Asia Pacific Journal of Management* 26(3): 435–457.

Roberts, J. Timmons and Nikki D. Thanos. 2003. *Trouble in Paradise: Globalization and Environmental Crises in Latin America*. Routledge: London & New York.

Roberts, J. Timmons, Bradley C. Parks and Alexis A. Vasquez. 2004. "Who Ratifies Environmental Treaties and Why? Institutionalism, Structuralism, and Participation by 192 Nations in 22 Treaties." *Global Environmental Politics* 4(3):22–64.

Rodrik, Dani. 2011. *The Globalization Paradox: Democracy and the Future of the World Economy*. New York: W.W. Norton & Company.

Roe, Mark. J. 2003. *Political Determinants of Corporate Governance: Political Context, Corporate Impact*. Oxford: Oxford University Press.

Running, Katrina. (2012) "Examining Environmental Concern in Developed, Transitioning and Developing Countries." *World Values Research* 5(1):1–25.

Sala-i-Martin, Xavier and Carlos Augusto Lopez. 2004. *The Global Competitiveness Report*. New York: Oxford University Press.

Schmidt, Vivien Ann. 2001. "The Politics of Adjustment in France and Britain: When Does Discourse Matter?" *Journal of European Public Policy* 8(2): 247–264.

Schmidt, Vivien Ann. 2002. *Futures of European Capitalism*. Oxford: Oxford University Press.

Schmidt, Vivien Ann. 2003. "French Capitalism: Transformed, and Yet Still a Third Variety," *Economy and Society* 32(4): 526–554.

Schneider, Ben R. 2009. "Hierarchical Market Economies and Varieties of Capitalism in Latin America." *Journal of Latin American Studies* 41(January): 553–575.

Schneider, Carsten Q. and Claudius Wagemann. 2006. "Reducing Complexity in Qualitative Comparative Analysis (QCA): Remote and Proximate Factors and the Consolidation of Democracy." *European Journal of Political Research* 45(5): 751–786.

Schneider, Carsten Q. and Claudius Wagemann. 2007. *Set-Theoretic Methods for the Social Sciences: A Guide to Qualitative Comparative Analysis*. Cambridge: Cambridge University Press.

Schneider, Carsten Q. and Claudius Wagemann. 2010. "Standards of Good Practice in Qualitative Comparative Analysis (QCA) and Fuzzy-Sets." *Comparative Sociology* 9(3): 397–418.

Schrank, Andrew. 2009. "Understanding Latin American Political Economy: Varieties of Capitalism or Fiscal Sociology?" *Economy and Society* 38(1): 53–61.

Schroeder, Miriam. 2009. "Clean Development Mechanism for Chinese Priorities." *The Journal of Environment Development* 18:4 (December): 371–394.

Scott, W. Robert. 1995. *Institutions and Organizations (Foundations of Oranizational Science)*. Thousand Oaks, CA: Sage.

Scott, W. Robert. 2001. *Institutions and Organizations*. Thousand Oaks, CA: Sage, second edition.

Seawright, Jason. 2005. "Qualitative Comparative Analysis vis-à-vis Regression (Symposium on Qualitative Comparative Analysis)." *Studies in Comparative International Development* 40(1): 3–26.

Shafik, Nemat. 1994. "Economic Development and Environmental Quality: An Econometric Analysis." *Oxford Economic Papers*, 46 (October): 757–773.

Shaw, Timothy, Andrew F. Cooper, and Agata Antkiewiczb. 2007. "Global and/or Regional Development at the Start of the 21st Century: China, India and (South) Africa." *Third World Quarterly* 28(7): 1255–1270.

Singh, Val and Susan Vinnicombe. 2005. "The 2004 Female FTSE Index and Women Directors." *Women In Management Review* 18(7): 349–358.

Skocpol, Theda. 1980. *States and Social Revolutions: A Comparative Analysis of France, Russia and China*. Cambridge: Cambridge University Press.

Smith, Adam. 1776. *An Inquiry into the Nature and Causes of the Wealth of Nations: In Three Volumes*. London: Strahan and Cadell and Davies.

Sovacool, Benjamin K. 2011. "The Policy Challenges of Tradable Credits: A Critical Review of Eight Markets." *Energy Policy* 39 (January): 575–585.

Stallings, Barbara and William Streeck. 1995. "Capitalisms in Conflict? The United States, Europe and Japan in the post-Cold War World." In *Global Change, Regional Response*, ed. Barbara Stallings. Cambridge: Cambridge University Press.

Standard and Poor. 2014. *Emerging Markets Index Website*. (http://us.spindices.com/regional-exposure/global/emerging).

Stavins, Robert N. 2001. *Experience with Market-Based Environmental Policy Instruments (Discussion Paper 01–58)*. Washington, DC: Resources for the Future.

Stern, David I. 2003. "The Environmental Kuznets Curve" in *World Development* 32(8): 1419–1439.

Stern, David I., Michael S. Common and Edward B. Barbier. 1996. "Economic Growth and Environmental Degradation: The Environmental Kuznets Curve and Sustainable Development." *World Development* 24: 1151–1160.

Stearns, Peter. 2013. *The Industrial Revolution in World History*. Philadelphia: Westview Press.

Storz, Cornelia, Bruno Amable, Steven Casper and Sebastien Lechevalier. 2013. "Bringing Asia into the Comparative Capitalism Perspective." *Socioeconomic Review* 11(2): 217–232.

Suri, Vivek and Duane Chapman.1998. "Economic Growth, Trade and the Energy: Implications for the Environmental Kuznets Curve." *Ecological Economics* 25: 195–208.

Tan, Justin and Yong Zeng. 2009. "A Stage-dependent Model of Resource Utilization, Strategic Flexibility, and Implications for Performance over Time: Empirical Evidence from a Transitional Environment." *Asia Pacific Journal of Management* 26(3): 563–588.

Terjesen, Siri and Jolanda Hessels. 2009. "Varieties of Export-oriented Entrepreneurship in Asia." *Asia Pacific Journal of Management* 26(3): 537–561.

Thelen, Kathleen. 2001. "Historical Institutionalism in Comparative Politics." *Annual Review of Political Science* 2(1): 369–404.

Tipton, Frank B. 2009. "Southeast Asian Capitalism: History, Institutions, States, and Firms." *Asia Pacific Journal of Management* 26(3): 401–434.

Tollefson, Jeff. 2010. "Ozone Treaty Could Be Used for Greenhouse Gases." *Nature* (November), doi:10.1038/news.2010.584.

UNEP Risø Centre. 2013. *CDM/JI Pipeline Analysis and Database*. UNEP Risø Centre, Capacity Development. (www.cdmpipeline.org/).

United Nations. 2011/2012. "Statistic Annex." In *The World Economic Situation and Prospects*, ed. Department of Economic and Social Affairs of the U.N. Secretariat. New York: United Nations Publications, 131–140.

United Nations Population Fund (UNFPA) Website. 2013. "Linking Population, Poverty and Development." (www.unfpa.org/pds/climate/).

U.S. Energy Information Administration. 2014. International Energy Outlook 2014: World Petroleum and Other Liquid Fuels. Report number: DOE/EIA-0484(2014). Washington, DC: Office of Integrated and International Energy Analysis (www.eia.gov/ieo).

U.S. Environmental Protection Agency (EPA). 2009. "Acid Rain Program 2007 Progress Report." EPA website on Clean Air Markets (January). (www.epa.gov/airmarkt/progress/arp07.html).

Vig, Norman J. and Michael E. Kraft. 2013. *Environmental Policy: New Directions for the Twenty-First Century*. Thousand Oaks, CA: CQ Press.

Vitols, Sigurt, ed. 2001. *Varieties of Capitalism: The Institutional Foundations of Comparative Advantage*. Oxford: Oxford University Press.

Vogel, Steven K. 2006. *Japan Remodeled: How Government and Industry Are Reforming Japanese Capitalism*. Ithaca: Cornell University Press

Wara, Michael. 2010. "Measuring the Clean Development Mechanism's Performance and Potential." In *Climate Change Science and Policy*, eds.Schneider, Stephen Henry, Armin Rosencranz, Michael D. Mastrandrea and Kristin Kuntz-Duriseti. Washington, DC: Island Press.

Walter, Andrew and Xiaoke Zhang, eds. 2012. *East Asian Capitalism: Diversity, Continuity and Change*. Oxford: Oxford University Press.

Weiss, Linda. 1998. *The Myth of the Powerless State: Governing the Economy in a Global Era*. Cambridge: Polity Press.

Whitley, Richard. 1992. *Business Systems in East Asia: Firms, Markets, and Societies*. London: Sage Publishers.

Whitley, Richard. 1994. *European Business Systems: Firms and Markets in Their National Contexts*. Newbury Park, CA: Sage Publishers.

Whitley, Richard. 1999. *Divergent Capitalisms: The Social Structuring and Change of Business Systems*. Oxford: Oxford University Press.

Wickham-Crowley, Timothy. 1991. "A Qualitative Comparative Approach to Latin American Revolutions." *International Journal of Comparative Sociology* XXXII(1–2): 82–108.

Williamson, Oliver. 1981. "The Economics of Organizations: The Transaction Cost Approach." *American Journal of Sociology* 87(November): 548–575.

Williamson, Oliver. 1985. *The Economic Institutions of Capitalism*. New York: Free Press.

Wong, Joseph. 2006. *Varieties of Capitalism in Asia: Health Industry Development in Korea, Singapore and Taiwan*. Presented at the American Political Science Association Annual Meeting, Philadelphia, PA.

World Bank. 2011. *Global Development Horizons 2011*. Washington, DC: World Bank Publications.

World Bank. 2012. *World Bank Development Indicators*. Washington, DC: World Bank Publications.

World Economic Forum. 2006/2012. *Global Risks 2012*. Cologne, Switzerland: World Economic Forum.

World Values Survey. 2013. *World Values Survey Data-Archive Online (2005–2008)*. (www.worldvaluessurvey.org/).

Yamamura, Kozo and William Streeck, eds. 2001. *The Origins of Nonliberal Capitalism: Germany and Japan in Comparison (Cornell Studies in Political Economy)*. Ithaca, NY: Cornell University.

Yandle, Bruce, Maya Vijayaraghavan and Madhusudan Bhattarai. 2000. "The Environmental Kuznets Curve: A Primer." Bozeman, Montana, PERC—the Property and Environment Research Center. (http://perc.org/articles/environmental-kuznets-curve).

Yeung, Henry Wai-Chung. 2000. "Organizing 'the Firm' in Industrial Geography I: Networks, Institutions and Regional Development." *Progress in Human Geography*. 24: 301–315.

Young, Oran. 1989. *International Cooperation: Building Regimes for Natural Resources and the Environment*. Ithaca: Cornell University Press.

Young, Oran. 2008. "Building Regimes for Socioecological Systems: Institutional Diagnostics." In *Institutions and Environmental Change: Principal Findings, Applications, and Research Frontiers*, eds. Oran R. Young, Leslie A. King and Heike Schroeder. Cambridge, MA: MIT Press, 115–143.

Young, Oran. 2012. "Navigating the Sustainability Transition: Governing Complex and Dynamic Socioecological Systems." In *Global Environmental Commons: Analytical and Political Challenges in Building Governance Mechanisms*, eds. Eric Brousseau, Tom Dedeurwaerdere, Pierre-André Jouvet, and Marc Willinger. Oxford: Oxford University Press, 80–101.

Young, Oran. 2013. "Navigating the Sustainability Transition: Governing Complex and Dynamic Socioecological Systems." In *Global Environmental Commons: Analytical and Political Challenges in Building Governance Mechanisms*, eds. Eric Brousseau, Tom Dedeurwaerdere, Pierre-André Jouvet and Marc Willinger. Oxford: Oxford University Press, 80–101.

Index

For Product Safety Concerns and Information please contact our EU
representative GPSR@taylorandfrancis.com
Taylor & Francis Verlag GmbH, Kaufingerstraße 24, 80331 München, Germany

www.ingramcontent.com/pod-product-compliance
Ingram Content Group UK Ltd.
Pitfield, Milton Keynes, MK11 3LW, UK
UKHW021300190926
475701UK00009B/87
* 9 7 8 1 1 3 8 2 8 7 2 9 7 *